God's Storehouse Principle

Sheila Holm

God's Storehouse Principle
Copyright © 2014 Sheila Holm

All rights reserved.

No part of this book may be reproduced,
stored in a retrieval system or transmitted in any form
or by any means whether by electronic, mechanical,
photocopying, recording or any other,
except for brief quotations in printed reviews
without the prior written permission
from the author.

ISBN-10:1495948544

ISBN-13:978-1495948541

Unless otherwise indicated all scriptures are taken from the
New King James version of the Bible.

HISBest4us@aol.com
Printed in USA by HIS Best Publishing

Dedication, In Grateful Acknowledgment

To the memory of my Father (1918-2011) who did not lose faith in the midst of crisis and always taught us to do the right thing and my Mother who has taught by example, Irvin and Clarice, and to my California family, my cousins LaVonne and Gene McGee, and to our ancestors who emigrated to America for religious freedom and stood firm in faith.

To Bishop George Dallas McKinney for the depth of prophetic understanding required, for being steadfast in helping me to keep on keepin' on, personally, encouraging me prior to and after each new adventure with God, while I remain grateful for your stand for all God sends to you!

To the memory (1918-2006) of Pastor Harald Bredesen, the friendship developed during meetings with and introductions arranged by him, especially for setting up my interview with Benny Hinn. For sharing front row studio seats because God orchestrated my attendance as a witness of the prophetic word from Benny Hinn that God would send a Muslim man with a salvation testimony and his name would be Nasir (Dr. Nasir Siddiki).

To Pastor Steve Dittmar, Jubilee Church, and to my host families during my visits, especially to Michael and Wendy Blomquist and to the powerful testimony of Christina Thee to confirm the faith level of children at four years old, and to her family for providing the Tommy Tenney books, plus to the many prayer partners and the multiple blessings received by participating at Jubilee after each assignment 'in a new way' as orchestrated by God.

To Pastor Earl Harrigan for being an amazing, anointed singer, especially **Walk on the Water** and **All Rise,** plus being a key witness to these days.

To John Willison for his mighty testimony and his offer to provide a tour of the TBN studio in Irving, Texas, a tour which has not happened, yet, however, it led to an introduction with the TBN producer, the opportunity to be interviewed on **Praise The Lord,** and for being the pilot who provided travel to a women's conference in Arkansas and to the Oklahoma church to encourage a pastor who was also from Nebraska. By the way, I'm still waiting for the promised tour of TBN.

To Big John Hall for confirming God introduced us at a Rodney Howard Browne meeting without sharing a word; God's plan when we were in each others' 'hometown.'

To Ken Blanchard, for understanding exactly where my life was and what was required to get me out from under the rock to stand firm on the rock once again while living beyond the 'world plans' by diving 100% into Kingdom business!

To Rodney Howard Browne for returning many times to San Diego at the exact time to renew the anointing that restores and prepares me to say YES for the next assignment.

To TD Jakes, Pastor Sam Ankrah and Pastor Charles Benneh and staff, to Bishop Duncan Williams and his worship team, to pastors & Bishops in London, especially Bishop John Francis for sharing the gift of his *Finally* CD, for the amazing contributions made during my journey.

To Pastor Mark Smallcomb for understanding the depth of **God's Storehouse Principle** message, yielding to God's structure, inviting me to share the details with business leaders and surrounding churches, including me within the Ed Silvoso meetings and for proclaiming the testimony of what God did when we came together on national TV (Australian version of CBS 60 Minutes).

To Pastor Rex Morgan for yielding to God so the Aboriginal Community could hear the message of **God's Storehouse Principle** and support the implementation during the service.

To Pastor Arnold in London for being so deeply touched by the message within **God's Storehouse Principle** that you were seeking the best of the best audio options to give me a copy so it would re-encourage me in the exact moment when I needed re-encouragement.

To Pastor Isileli for capturing **God's Storehouse Principle** before gathering the church together for fasting and prayer and remaining diligent until God confirmed it was time for us to meet together for God would change a nation if we stood firm together with our Lord.

To Prophet and Apostle John Kelly for prophetic words over my life and for referring me to Pastor Harold Dewberry.

To Pastor Harold Dewberry for standing firm, delivering and releasing so many from what binds their heart and mind and returns them to a real relationship with Christ, for fasting and praying until God shared a clear message about me traveling down under and remaining in the country long enough for God to orchestrate the time and opportunity for me to meet with the Pastor in Fiji, a trip which unfolded weeks after you left your laptop with me and returned to America.

To the many pastors, evangelists, teachers, and fellow prophets and apostles, and the leadership of the church, the speakers and saints participating in the various seminars and conferences around the world who have invited me, encouraged me, prayed with me and introduced me to host families who have become part of my breath of life gift from God. To Kirk & Joni Bovill for their music, to the prayer partners, intercessors and prayer warriors walking the wall: Calvin Jackson, Paul Davis, Carol Marfori, Lisa Hauri, to the memory of Jan Franklin (leaving us too soon, December 7, 2008), a powerful prayer warrior who walked the wall and joined me as a witness for all of the California meetings and she became a valued prayer assistant with the long prayer lines, to Gary & Cindy Graham and to the memory (1953-2011) of 'Rozi' Graham Blegen, because in our lives as we gather together *It's A Faith Walk!* with the Holy Spirit confirming our personal part within *God's Storehouse Principle.*

TABLE OF CONTENTS

		PAGE
Foreword by Bishop George Dallas McKinney		9
Prologue		11
Introduction		23
Chapter 1	Storehouse	29
Chapter 2	Understanding	41
Chapter 3	Blessings	49
Chapter 4	Perspective	61
Chapter 5	Wake-up Call	87
Chapter 6	Expand Time!	99
Chapter 7	Store Time	111
Chapter 8	Tithe Time	129
Chapter 9	Cash Flow	137
Chapter 10	Planning	147
Chapter 11	Talents, Skills, Abilities	153
Chapter 12	People, Network, Resources	157
Chapter 13	The Game; Balanced Life	167
Chapter 14	Discipleship	173
Epilogue		193
About the Author		199
Wigglesworth's Sermon: Dare To Believe, Then Command		211
America Founded upon Faith; Path to Freedom and Liberty		221

Freedom Monument: Wikipedia. National Monument to the Forefathers; Please view the DVD *Monumental* for further details. www.monumentalmovie.com. Kirk Cameron embarks upon the Pilgrim's journey from England to America. It will deepen your faith. Friends are buying DVD copies of *Monumental* for their family and friends.

Foreword

Sheila Holm has produced a concise statement on God's seeding and harvesting "Kingdom Business" principle - a tithe of all - as God's master plan for stewardship, while she shares how she discovered *God's Storehouse Principle*.

Sheila's journey of faith begins with the recognition that "we are totally and absolutely dependent upon God" and that God has predestined our lives for his purpose and provided a plan for us, which supports his work.

Armed with this knowledge and faith, Sheila becomes a yielded vessel to be God's ambassador to encourage Christians, especially pastors, throughout the US, Africa, Australia and Europe. Without sponsors or any visible means of support, she has traveled the world sustained by the faithfulness of God.

God's Storehouse Principle confirms God's wisdom and plan within the testimony, "*God supplies all that we are and all that we need and He requests that we bring tithes of all that He gives us...*" based on the truth "*...the Earth is the Lords and the Fullness thereof,*" Psalms 24:1-2, I Corinthians 10:26 and 28.

Since God is the owner of everything He has the right to establish the terms of stewardship imposed upon those entrusted with His property including all that we have been given: our life, time, treasure and talents. When *God's*

Storehouse Principle is implemented, while we unite together, for each other, *"All of God's work done God's way will not lack God's supply."*

God's Storehouse Principle is based upon God's plan that our blessings are to be shared so that the needs of others will be met, especially widows and orphans (all without husbands and fathers).

I strongly recommend *God's Storehouse Principle* for it is a timely and urgent call for every Christian to do all of our business God's way.

Bishop George Dallas McKinney

President, Pentecostal & Charismatic Churches North America (70,000+)

Board Member of Global Ministries: Billy Graham, Morris Cerullo, etc.

General Board Member, Church of God in Christ (COGIC)

Bishop and Pastor, St. Stephens Cathedral (COGIC)

Prologue

God's Storehouse Principle was revealed again and again by God within every experience during the three years while He orchestrated everything in my life. Rarely did He arrange for me to be home longer than the moments of time required to re-pack for the next assignment(s). Each time God orchestrated an invitation for me to preach, the theme of the message was the same: ***God's Storehouse Principle.*** At first, I did not feel qualified or worthy to be the one to bring the message to the Body of Christ even after the powerful prophetic word repeated often: ***As the mouse to the elephant you will be able to get the Body of Christ to move!*** As I rested, God's urgency prompted me to issue ***It's A Faith Walk!***

When the cover design was 'in question' God directed me to You Tube. This was a first. God wanted me to look for my name on You Tube. A surprise met with some excitement but, also some resistance. Why? I know there is nothing about me on You Tube. However, God was going to confirm to me that the book cover I thought would be right was right. Very first option stated a Sheila was going on a journey to find Coleridge the poet. It is also the name of my High School. The cover photo of the video regarding her journey was an identical match to the book cover I selected.

The moment the cover was approved, I experienced a birthing experience; pains plus symptoms were included. I've not had a family so I had no idea what was going on. Pains were extreme. Even though they left for a while they returned with greater intensity and for longer periods of time. There is more to this experience which can be shared at a later time.

Bottom line: Google medical response to the symptoms: *"You may not know you are pregnant but, you are giving birth."* Clearly I was pregnant with the details but I was not having a child. The experience confirmed the book was 'enough' and therefore the first release was 320 pages vs the planned 156 pages.

After the release, it felt like it was time to take a rest. However, God knows far more than I do about His timing. God was prompting me again and again with dreams and visions regarding the need to release what He has shared through me often: ***God's Storehouse Principle.***

As I reviewed the nearly 156 pages and made a few explanatory additions (little inserts, really) the book quickly grew to over 250 pages and it appeared it was going toward 320, also. So, I stopped. I prayed. I asked God to help me reduce the information to the bite sized pieces as He did it for me during the journeys and with the business book: ***Seven Step Business* Plan.** Plus, I needed God's help to quicken the process vs. the reading of it to feel like my years of training.

Preparation was God's response.

When I asked for clarity, God confirmed the people's hearts have to be prepared to comprehend ***God's Storehouse Principle.***

When I asked what would be the best way to prepare the hearts of the people, God responded: **Love.**

As God confirms in His word, no matter what gifts we might possess the greatest gift is love.

1 Corinthians 13:1-13. The Greatest Gift

Though I speak with the tongues of men and of angels, but have not love, I have become sounding brass or a clanging cymbal. 2 And though I have *the gift of* prophecy, and understand all mysteries and all knowledge, and though I have all faith, so that I could remove mountains, but have not love, I am nothing. 3 And though I bestow all my goods to feed *the poor,* and though I give my body to be burned, but have not love, it profits me nothing.

4 Love suffers long *and* is kind; love does not envy; love does not parade itself, is not puffed up; 5 does not behave rudely, does not seek its own, is not provoked, thinks no evil; 6 does not rejoice in iniquity, but rejoices in the truth; 7 bears all things, believes all things, hopes all things, endures all things.

8 Love never fails. But whether *there are* prophecies, they will fail; whether *there are* tongues, they will cease; whether *there is* knowledge, it will vanish away. 9 For we know in part and we prophesy in part. 10 But when that which is perfect has come, then that which is in part will be done away.

11 When I was a child, I spoke as a child, I understood as a child, I thought as a child; but when I became a man, I put away childish things. 12 For now we see in a mirror, dimly, but then face to face. Now I know in part, but then I shall know just as I also am known.

13 And now abide faith, hope, love, these three; but the greatest of these *is* love.

Immediately, an old saying came to mind:

> Oh Lord to be with you above,
> Now that will be the glory,
> But Lord, while I'm still here below
> With these Saints I know,
> Oh Lord, that's a different story!

Where Do We Find Our Example of Expressing Love?

1. God, the Father

"What is your relationship with your earthly father?"

I thought this was an odd question from a person who barely knew me. However, he was quite serious and he told me to take time thinking about the specific description because it makes a huge difference.

The best way I could describe my father at that time. Being Norwegian is the reason why he said he is quieter than most. We did talk this question and experience after I gave it some thought and our relationship changed for the better after this experience:

1. Cares deeply,

2. Retains peace, to the point of avoiding conflict,

3. Quiet, reserved; often provides one word answers,

4. Does not share his heart very often,

5. Rarely, if ever, does he initiate a conversation,

6. Can hear a full day of conversation even during a family reunion and then summarize all of it within a phrase or a sentence,

7. Loyal and devoted to the family even if he is not honored for his sacrifices.

Important that I not spoil your surprise in doing this exercise for yourself. Please take a moment and list your top seven:

1.

2.

3.

4.

5.

6.

7.

Then, the man merely asked:

"What is your relationship with your heavenly Father?"

Wow, I had not thought about a relationship with God. Up to this point, I hoped I pleased God. I hoped I was doing what was good in His sight.

Important that I not spoil your surprise in doing this exercise for yourself. Please take a moment and list your top seven:

1.

2.

3.

4.

5.

6.

7.

My experience. As I thought about the time I spent with God, I knew I could confirm that He:

1. Cares deeply,

2. Retains peace, does not express conflict,

3. Quiet, reserved; sometimes I might hear one word,

4. Does not share His heart with me,

5. Rarely, if ever, has He initiated a conversation,

6. He hears me chatter on and on, while the most I was hearing from Him was a phrase or maybe a sentence,

7. He has been loyal to me even when I have not honored Him for His sacrifices.

This was an eye opener!

I had no idea that we think human and that causes us to limit God and how we perceive His love for us & that becomes the way we view our relationship. How we think and limit our thoughts and abilities to be in relationship with others is often the result of how we were when we were relating to our father. It was a shock to see the exact same thoughts 'in print' but there it was in my own words laid out before me in black and white.

God's love for us is beyond human comprehension.

John 3:16 & 17. For God so loved the world that He gave His only begotten Son, that whoever believes in Him should not perish but have everlasting life. [17] For God did not send His Son into the world to condemn the world, but that the world through Him might be saved.

Often, God prompts me to tell a person in a prayer line: ***"God loves you so much He sent His Son."*** It's powerful!

2. God, the Son

Jesus confirmed how we are to be and to pray. He gave us the Lord's Prayer: Our Father, who art in heaven, Hallowed be thine name … thy kingdom come … thy will be done on earth as it is in heaven …

Jesus did as His Father; always about His Father's business:

John 8:28-30. Then Jesus said to them, *"When you lift up the Son of Man, then you will know that I am He, and that I do nothing of Myself; but as My Father taught Me, I speak these things.* [29] *And He who sent Me is with Me. The Father has not left Me alone, for I always do those things that please Him."* [30] As He spoke these words, many believed in Him.

John 4: 10. A Samaritan Woman Meets Her Messiah

Jesus answered and said to her, *"If you knew the gift of God, and who it is who says to you, 'Give Me a drink,' you would have asked Him, and He would have given you living water."*

John 4:34. Disciples concern; Jesus had no food to eat

Jesus said to them, *"My food is to do the will of Him who sent Me, and to finish His work.*

Grasping God's plan for our life, with Christ as the example can seem impossible, but as God reminded me when he took my hand: ...with God all things are possible!

John 14: 19-24. Indwelling of the Father and the Son

"A little while longer and the world will see Me no more, but you will see Me. Because I live, you will live also. [20] At that day you will know that I *am* in My Father, and you in Me, and I in you. [21] He who has My commandments and keeps them, it is he who loves Me. And he who loves Me will be loved by My Father, and I will love him and manifest Myself to him."

[22] Judas said to Him, "Lord, how is it that You will manifest Yourself to us, and not to the world?"

[23] Jesus answered and said to him, "If anyone loves Me, he will keep My word; and My Father will love him, and We will come to him and make Our home with him. [24] He who does not love Me does not keep My words; and the word which you hear is not Mine but the Father's who sent Me.

3. God, the Holy Spirit

John 16:5-15. The Work of the Holy Spirit

"But now I go away to Him who sent Me, and none of you asks Me, 'Where are You going?' [6] But because I have said these things to you, sorrow has filled your heart. [7] Nevertheless I tell you the truth. It is to your advantage that I go away; for if I do not go away, the Helper will not come to you; but if I depart, I will send Him to you. [8] And when He has come, He will convict the world of sin, and of righteousness, and of judgment: [9] of sin, because they do not believe in Me; [10] of righteousness, because I go to My Father and you see Me no more; [11] of judgment, because the ruler of this world is judged.

¹² "I still have many things to say to you, but you cannot bear *them* now. ¹³ However, when He, the Spirit of truth, has come, He will guide you into all truth; for He will not speak on His own *authority,* but whatever He hears He will speak; and He will tell you things to come. ¹⁴ He will glorify Me, for He will take of what is Mine and declare *it* to you. ¹⁵ All things that the Father has are Mine. Therefore I said that He will take of Mine and declare *it* to you.

John 14: 25-28.The Gift of His Peace

"These things I have spoken to you while being present with you. ²⁶ But the Helper, the Holy Spirit, whom the Father will send in My name, He will teach you all things, and bring to your remembrance all things that I said to you. ²⁷ Peace I leave with you, My peace I give to you; not as the world gives do I give to you. Let not your heart be troubled, neither let it be afraid. ²⁸ You have heard Me say to you, 'I am going away and coming *back* to you.' If you loved Me, you would rejoice because I said, 'I am going to the Father,' for My Father is greater than I.

God's Love Surpasses Human Understanding

God loves us so much, He sent His Son.

After Jesus Christ gave His life for our sins, He promised to send a guide so we would know through the Holy Spirit that the Father and Son will be with us always.

Knowing you are loved, deeply, and with the Holy Spirit guiding each step according to what God and Jesus Christ are saying what we are to know and do in the moment, we know that we know we are loved and never alone. Praying for the immediate release of all limiting thoughts and all of the lies of the enemy as you begin to understand, act upon and become blessed by living your life according to *God's Storehouse Principle.*

Until I hear your testimonies due to what is revealed to you as you read the words and hear the Lord speak to you, so deeply you even hear His whispers, you can trust that I pray you will continue to experience HIS Best!

Sheila

Email: hisbest4usorders@gmail.com
Web site: http://hisbest4us.org
Use the subject line: **God's Storehouse Principle.**

Introduction: *God's Storehouse Principle*
Also Known As (aka) *God's Storehouse Principle*
In 60 Seconds

OK. You cannot blame me. This is something God wanted me to add 'at the last minute.' It's not my fault! Really!

God has a fabulous sense of humor that surpasses what I would have imagined before we embarked on the three year journey around the world.

As the final edits are being made to this book, God has prompted me to insert a 60 second commercial type of structure in the beginning due to what has happened to us within the current generation: *We want to know about it, have it prepared for us and served to us within seconds.*

And, the Kendrick Brothers / Sherwood Pictures have added a special section to their DVDs: **Facing the Giants** and **Courageous,** where they take us through the entire movie within 60 seconds. I'm laughing the entire time. However, I'm not sure this addition will be as enjoyable for you or as their visual edtion!

Briefly, this is what *God's Storehouse Principle* is all about:

1. God's word is true. Whatever we hear from whatever authority at whatever time in life, we need to check the message we hear with God's word before we proceed.

2. God's commandments are specific. The blessings flow when we help each other keep the commandments.

I have to insert a little note about the *History of the World: Part I* movie clip (available on You Tube) with Mel Brooks (screenwriter and director) as an actor playing Moses. As Moses dropped the first set of tablets, as he's bringing three tablets of The Commandments down the mountain he slips as he announces 15 commandments; one tablet falls and breaks. He immediately states: 10 commandments. Adorable, but people now ask if there really were 15. God had to make a second set of the 10!

3. God's church is built upon the apostles (structure) and prophets (word) with Christ as the Chief Cornerstone. The structure is five-fold but, we put all pressure and responsibilty upon the some who are called to be pastors! Shame on us!

4. God's requests are honored:

- Go forth and disciple, share God's word / truth with the people in our life every chance we get,
- Feed the lambs, also known as (aka) help those in need by discipling them while they are learning and maturing,
- Especially meet the needs and care for the widows (and, the women without husbands) and the orphans (and, the children without fathers), and
- Share the blessings of all God has provided to us and seeded within us (our talents, skills and abilities, plus our

resources), so none shall leave the assembly in lack. Live life abundantly (and balanced) and prosper!

5. God's protection to live free due to our salvation through the sacrifice and blood of Jesus and our deliverance from the enemy is supported by the guidance of the Holy Spirit and by putting on the full Armor of God so we can stand firm. In fact, so we can stand firm against the powers and principalities even before we put on the armor.

6. Align our life with God's will so it will become on Earth as it is in Heaven.

7. Love those our LORD sends to us, sharpening each other as iron sharpens iron and disciple the nations (people) with the LORD's truth while bringing them to the feet of Jesus.

If this is already how the body of Christ is functioning within your life, family, neighborhood and region then the people you have surrounded yourself with are already operating per *God's Storehouse Principle.*

God provided the truth within the structure I am briefly sharing within this book and to help us get from where we are to where we need to be, I'm providing the structure within a workbook so you can 'fill in the blanks' and have a life of peace which is in balance. Until we are living a blessed life, it is not easy to comprehend how to help others live blessed.

What Are We to Bring to the Storehouse?

God wants you whieh is everything God has seeded within you and provided for you and to you to be a blessing to you, to those in your family and sphere of influence in your nation and beyond.

In scripture, God asks us for a tithe of all of the increase from us. God did not say it is all about money. You do not find God asking you to bring your money to the church or pledge an amount of money based upon what you think your future income might be.

God wants and needs us to understand the tithe is a tithe of all that we are for that is the representation of all that He has seeded within us and to us. Some were and are farmers, and their tithe of the increase is based on grains, animals & produce.

God's people have need of all that God has provided to us, whether we are attorneys or auto mechanics, drivers to appointments or dentists, store keepers or bakers, etc. , etc., etc.

God needs us to become His people who will help fill His Storehouse with a tithe of all He has granted to us, giving from our increase / blessings so the storehouse will function properly with the people being blessed and their needs being met.

If the storehouse is not functioning properly and this status is not the case in your life, family and community, God's truth in these pages will bless you deeply for it is God's desire that we live free, protected and abundantly blessed.

God's plan does seem as simple as it is stated above because He knows the 'living it day by day in the world' is another situation altogether! Herein lies the issue of love and gaining balance!

If the simple structure was our reality regarding how our life is being lived today within our relationships, families and communities, what we would see as 'the church' would look much different. Christians would be living and proceeding according to the truth in God's word as the churches of Corinth, Philippi, etc., the same structure God has shown me, a structure which helps us 'keep life in balance'.

Opportunity to Wake-up & Become the Church!

It is painful to hear so many people state the church, the body of Christ, is still in the pre-toddler phase and not walking as disciples, discipling others, yet.

Many people are crying out to the Lord, hoping to hear the truth. They hear a good word on Sunday and hope it will carry them through the week.

Trusting this is why God has shown me so much about what He has planned for us and <u>why we need to operate as bible based and spirit-filled believers</u>. The first time I heard that, I did not know the difference between the churches or what it would be like to be in a church which is bible based and spirit-filled.

When I found out, I was richly blessed!

Without God's guidance, as directed by the Holy Spirit, we lack the ability to comprehend or act upon God's plan for our lives. I pray you will lean on God's word and gain His guidance throughthe Holy Spirit and not lean on your own or man's understanding or interpretation for it will take a lot of us letting go of what we think we know to gain the LORD's truth and get this body of Christ to move forward. To do that, we have to be able to hear the truth directly from God so we can unite together and proceed with God in doing Kingdom work so it shall be on earth as it is in heaven exactly as Jesus taught us to pray.

Due to how the church is structured 'in the world' today as a one-fold ministry with all responsibilty held by the pastor vs. how God told us to structure the church within the bible, we are about 180 degrees off course. We have compromised with the world so much the church does not resemble the structure God provided.

To change this status, we need to immediately shift our plans from world based plans to functioning within ***God's Storehouse Principle.*** To do this, we have to shift our focus to His word!

Bottom line: We have to realize the commission is to go forth and disciple so the people know the truth. This means the body will come to know how much God loves them . When they express God's love and blessings showered upon their life, they will be ready to disciple others. The people who hear their testimony will realize how much God loves them and disciple others in the truth and so on, and so on. To do this, the church has to shift nearly 180 degrees from the current course. # 1 As a body of Christ, the church has to stop asking the people to meet the needs of the church! May we become a people who gather together, declare God's blessings poured out upon us, the fellowship of believers, and focus upon sharing all that we have & who we are with those in need so none shall leave the assembly or live their life in lack.

Chapter 1   God's Storehouse Principle: Storehouse

If you usually start a book at Chapter 1 and you skipped Prologue and Introduction, please go back to page 27 because our journey is based upon our personal relationship with God and you will want to process the information in the Prologue before you proceed upon this journey. Thanks!

In *It's A Faith Walk!* I shared a few details about God sending me on a special journey while I was in England which became known as *The Search for Wigglesworth.*

Prior to the journey, God was focused upon the theme of His Storehouse so it was tearful when God revealed the physical 'storehouse' which used to be built next to the church. The Storehouse became the location and expression of the tithe of all of the 'increase' / blessings upon the people to share and bless those in the ministry and all in need.

This creates a different conversation in the church than the conversation about tithing money today for the needs of the church vs. sharing testimonies as we share the blessings with the people, the desire of the LORD for us to 'feed the lambs', especially the widows (without husbands) and orphans (without fathers).

Lord, What's a Storehouse?

Hold on to the arms of your chair for you are ready for the ride of your life: time travel, so to speak.

Back in time, the people brought the 'tithe of their increase' of their grain, livestock and produce so all in need are cared for, as God asks the church to feed the lambs with food and the truth, and to especially care for the widows and the orphans. The fellowship of believers shared and were encouraged when the people brought a tithe of all they are and of their 'increase' from all that was harvested (wisdom and grain) in that week, so there would be 'enough' for the priest / pastor and those in need, especially the widows and the orphans.

If it became too much, if the load was too heavy to bring it to the church it was OK to sell the items of the tithe offering in the marketplace and bring the money provided from the sale to help provide for the needs from all that was provided within the storehouse.

The storehouse used to be alive and well in the churches around the world. However, the storehouse and planning the tithe of the increase both appear to be missing in the church.

The storehouses are no longer built next to the church building, and only cash has been considered 'tithe' from the people. And, per most churches, the people are asked to make a pledge in advance. This is called 'good stewardship' for the people to promise the church a tithe of cash from the full amount of future income before it is earned and available before the income is 'in hand' or prayed about before it is contributed. This bypasses the tithe process: blessings realized, prayed over and shared after received.

Wow. This opens the door wide for the enemy.

Any auto maintenance or health issue that arises will cause a problem for the family being unable to 'meet the agreed upon pledge / commitment made in advance as a tithe.' It removes all of the time we are to spend with God reviewing the 'blessings / increase' and seeking how God would have us tithe of who we are and what we have.

This is more critical due to the lack of testimonies regarding God's blessings, based upon God's provision. It shifts our conversation to a confirmation of man's provision of income for a job as there are fewer and fewer people raising grains, animals and produce or providing food for the people in need, and nobody seems to know what the widows and orphans need as it is typically left up to the structure of the various government programs.

Lord forgive us for we have done things which allowed compromising with the plans of the world / the enemy, while we knew not what we were allowing or doing or that we were turning our back on You while heading in the wrong direction by neglecting Your word!

It was tearful during the vision God shared which confirmed the pastors are often preaching about the people needing to meet the needs of the church. This preaching / teaching keeps the body of Christ living in poverty / lack vs. declaring the blessings as the people are not sharing testimonies about the blessings they have received which result in sharing with the fellowship so they are not confirming they are experiencing the receipt of blessings. Therefore, they do not have testimonies to share. When I am asked to preach, I ask the people to share their testimonies and trying to get one or two people to come forward is not easy!

The people are either not aware of the blessings / provision as they relate to their prayers seeking God's provision or they did not prepare a tithe from the 'increase' in their lives.

God knows the plans He has for each of us, plans to prosper us, and God will share the plans with all who have ears to hear and eyes to see the blessings available to share with others as ***God's Storehouse Principle*** is outlined within the bible. God's orchestration and provision cycle requires our full participation. When we align with God's plan, the blessings will flow amongst people and the focus upon money for more buildings will disappear from being the conversation. I've been a witness to this in many of the churches where I have been asked to preached.

God keeps it very simple. God's currency fulfills dreams and plans. The world's currency exists in a constant state of lack. We have made it complex. How? We have compromised with the world so often over time and in so many areas of life, the church does not resemble the church per God's structure. The money focus has affected every aspect of the church and the lives of the people.

In **John 10:10,** *Jesus confirmed that He came so that we might have life, and have it more abundantly!*

God has shown me that we are about 180 degrees off course and to get the body of Christ back on track, we have to come back to His word, His structure and truth as believers, the Body of Christ. Our focus has to shift about everything!

To do it, we have to know how we can individually help the body of Christ resolve the 180 degree difference. God's word, God's wisdom is the answer.

Since we are about 180 degrees off the original course and 'it is our shift' on earth to help it become as it is in heaven, and since it is becoming obvious to us during our generation that something is wrong the responsibility is ours to turn this ship (the body of Christ) back around. To make it happen, we need to unite together & proceed per God's guidance. A good visual to help us has been shared as an email message. I've seen this cycle through a few times. It is just as meaningful as a reminder as it was the first time

I read it. It is powerful because it includes the definition of the Holy Spirit's Guidance as the process of G (God) U (you) and I in a DANCE. I've searched many sources to provide the entire structure for you and the words are always credited to an unknown author and yet, they remain identical within both ministry and research / resource web sites: Author unknown.

Guidance: *You & I in a DANCE with God*

When I meditated on the word GUIDANCE, I kept seeing 'dance' at the end of the word. I remember reading that doing God's will is a lot like dancing.

When two people try to lead, nothing feels right. The movement doesn't flow with the music, and everything is quite uncomfortable and jerky.

When one person realizes that, and lets the other lead, both bodies begin to flow with the music. One gives gentle cues, perhaps with a nudge to the back or by pressing lightly in one direction or another. It's as if two become one body, moving beautifully. The dance takes surrender, willingness, and attentiveness from one person and gentle guidance and skill from the other.

My eyes drew back to the word GUIDANCE.

When I saw "G," I thought of God, followed by "U" and "I." "God, "U" and "I" dance. God, you, and I dance. As I lowered my head, I became willing to trust that I would get guidance about my life. Once again, I became willing to let God lead.

My prayer for you today is that God's blessings and mercies be upon you on this day and everyday. May you abide in God as God abides in you. Dance together with God, trusting God to lead and to guide you through each season of your life. This prayer is powerful and there is nothing attached. If God has done anything for you in your life, please share this message with someone else, for prayer is one of the best gifts we can receive. There is no cost but a lot of rewards; so let's continue to pray for one another AND I HOPE YOU DANCE!

The message is similar to the country song *I Hope You Dance* confirms: ***Promise me that you'll give faith a fighting chance and when you get the choice to sit it out or dance, I hope you dance!***

This is my prayer for us, also: ***I hope we learn to dance!***

Forgive Us Father For We Knew Not What We Did

Lord, as Your sheep You desire for us to know Your voice and to be led by the Holy Spirit and to structure Your church according to Your word, but, we were not discipled so we did not know and we did not disciple. We did not know how to establish the body of Christ founded upon the apostles and prophets with Christ as the Chief Cornerstone so we did not proceed as the church was established with the fellowship of believers in Ephesus, Corinth, etc. Over time, we have not been equipped and trained. Instead, without realizing what was happening to the body of Christ we started leaning upon our own / man's / enemy's understanding by following man's plan. The churches were established for us to follow the doctrine of man, the leaders / pastors / shepherd's and we trusted it was Your plan for us without checking the plans as they are defined within Your word. Oh Lord, we realize now that we got off track. The requests of the leaders are for the people to meet the needs of the church structire instead of the church (us) blessing the believers who gather to fellowship in Your name and those you direct us to bless. Keep Your hand upon us while we refocus our eyes upon You, open our ears to hear You, align with Your word and submit to Your guidance through the counsel of the Holy Spirit. Help us learn how to dance with You, Lord. Amen!

Personal Perspective

In *It's A Faith Walk* I shared the story about being so upset with God because I was leaving a conference in Northern California with an empty tank of gas, without the promised blessing which was going to be shared and it would be an amount beyond the rental car and gas. I was still upset even though God filled the tank while I was driving and while He kept the tank full for the journey (brought me home on the same tank of gas vs buying 2.5 tanks of gas), and God continued to keep the tank full for the next journey (another 2-3 tanks of gas), after God shared a message about **preparing His Army, calling forth the women, even His widows and orphans for the men are not putting on their steel toed boots and preparing to march before the SONrise.**

When I shared the word from God with the man, he said, **"God's righteousness precedes you, showers over you and follows you like a mighty wake ..."** He's the same man who shared the mouse to the elephant vision and he said God showed him to be a man who is satisfied to gnaw on the ankle of the elephant, but I was not. God showed him how I was running and shouting and biting until the elephant moved. What a vision it must have been!

He told me the elephant is the body of Christ. He added that God confirmed I do get 'the body of Christ' to move. He said this vision was a confirmation that we are to meet again and I was thrilled, because it was true for me as God confirmed the message exactly in the moment while he was stating it and it was shared with me exactly three months after a young boy in Australia brought a picture for me to a meeting that God asked him draw the day before: A mouse on top of the elephant while moving forward!

This was even more exciting because there was a glorious moment during the conference which we did not act upon, yet. While we were at the conference, I shared a vision from God about the apostles gathering together in the 'war room' or 'situation room' as the military leaders do in America within the Pentagon or the White House.

The man confirmed God had shared the same vision with him, He had a military background and he knew it was in the pentagon and God even drew his attention to the exact same structure of the room and the exact same furniture as the LORD shared in the vision with me.

I waited for more confirmations from the Lord while I actually resisted sharing any of the information at that time or since due to the fact I am merely one servant of the most high God.

I've only seen the experience of God's righteousness showering over someone one more time and I shared it while I was speaking with him just a few days ago. I pray God will touch his heart and your heart, and the hearts of the people who God knows will help get this body of Christ to wake-up, align and move forward!

In fact, tears flowed each time God arranged for me to return to America, He showed me the extensive deterioration within the body of Christ, especially the inability of the people within the body to be able to discern His voice and to stand firm in large part due to the lack of knowledge.

Hosea 4:6

My people are destroyed for lack of knowledge. Because you have rejected knowledge, I also will reject you from being priest for Me; Because you have forgotten the law of your God, I also will forget your children.

Lord, help us know who we are and how to proceed in truth.

\# 1 The church is not established as God told us to establish the structure: Upon the Apostles and Prophets with Christ as the Chief Cornerstone.

Ephesians 2:19-21

Now, therefore, you are no longer strangers and foreigners, but fellow citizens with the saints and members of the household of God, [20] having been built on the foundation of the apostles and prophets, Jesus Christ Himself being the chief corner*stone*, [21] in whom the whole building, being fitted together, grows into a holy temple in the Lord, [22] in whom you also are being built together for a dwelling place of God in the Spirit.

Instead of equipping and training the people, a different plan unfolded. Instead of building the church upon God's structure, as Paul did with the Ephesians, Corinthians, Philippians, etc., the people are only hearing from the pastors of the church who have become responsible for the full five-fold ministry. Shame on us! The various churches are being directed by man's or the world's structure within denominations established by man and the request for tithes includes paying for layers of the administration levels of the denominations. This is what has resulted in the shift of focus regarding the tithe to bless the workers in the ministry and the people in need to becoming a tithe by the people to submit money and pledge future income to meet the needs of **man's** church. The church has become a structure which depends upon man's budgets and not guided by the LORD.

Proverbs 3:4-6

And so find favor and high esteem in the sight of God and man. ⁵ Trust in the Lord with all your heart, And lean not on your own understanding; ⁶ In all your ways acknowledge Him, And He shall direct your paths.

We were not to lean upon our own understanding, man's understanding, the understanding of the world, we are to proceed per God's word.

We are to operate based upon God's word and proceed with the guidance of the Holy Spirit so we are sure we are taking our steps based upon God's wisdom and not our own understanding.

When we gather together, the apostles and prophets impart the wisdom of God and the gifts as guided by the Holy Spirit, as Paul established the churches and visited to re-encourage the saints. While traveling to Rome he sent this letter:

Romans 1:1, 2, 7-12, 16-17.

Greeting from Paul, called *to be* an apostle, separated to the gospel of God ² which He promised before through His prophets in the Holy Scriptures ... [7] To all who are in Rome, beloved of God, called *to be* saints:Grace to you and peace from God our Father and the Lord Jesus Christ.

Desire to Visit Rome. [8] First, I thank my God through Jesus Christ for you all, that your faith is spoken of throughout the whole world. [9] For God is my witness, whom I serve with my spirit in the gospel of His Son, that without ceasing I make mention of you always in my prayers, [10] making request if, by some means, now at last I may find a way in the will of God to come to you. [11] For I long to see you, that I may impart to you some spiritual gift, so that you may be established— [12] that is, that I may be encouraged together with you by the mutual faith both of you and me.

The Just Live by Faith. [16] For I am not ashamed of the gospel of Christ, for it is the power of God to salvation for everyone who believes, for the Jew first and also for the Greek. [17] For in it the righteousness of God is revealed from faith to faith; as it is written, "The just shall live by faith."

Bottom line: The church today is not operating per God's plan of the five-fold ministry within the fellowship, founded upon the apostles and prophets with Christ as the Chief Cornerstone. God kept it simple. He makes some to be apostles, prophets, evangelists, pastors and teachers. Each time the people within the church have proceeded 'per man' and compromised with the world whether with or without their full knowledge as a body of believers we have become more aligned with the world than with our LORD and over time this has caused the body of Christ, those who fellowship together as the church, to become more aligned with the world and therefore the church as God structured it to proceed is not represented in many of the churches today. *LORD forgive us, do not hold this against us for we lacked Your wisdom.*

Chapter 2   God's Storehouse Principle: Understanding

Lord, Help Us Know Who We Are In Christ!

A dear prayer partner, Jan Franklin, repeatedly sent an email to me with the headlines which would keep me awake and moving forward:

You are more than a conqueror.
Remember, you are the head and not the tail.
Your enemy is under your feet.

She knew that I was not hearing positive scriptures on a regular basis. The scriptures of 'correction' were typically the focus and I do thank God I've remained open to correction. However, constant correction put me on a different path. I was not hearing confirmations that God had any plans for me. In an effort to 'be nice' and 'be and do good things', I got off track. Without realizing it, I was merely focused upon helping people and doing good works. People who met me did not know for sure that Christ resided in my heart. I did not understand. I was shocked.

Without discipleship, equipping and training, I was merely hearing more instructions and things about me which I needed to fix, adjust, re-think before I would be 'of any value' to God. Years of sitting in a pew Sunday after Sunday. When God reached out and grabbed my hand, the 'on the job training' included a lot of denominational and religious thought removal to align with the LORD. Thank God we serve a God who is the same yesterday, today and tomorrow! He does not leave or forsake us!

I knew I needed God in my life.

I did not know God needed me.

So many within the body of Christ are waiting for God to do it all! Many confirm God will do it if God wants it done. However, God has confirmed the truth: *We are here to fulfill upon the plan and purpose God has for our life! There may not be one more person walking in faith to meet with and heal the person God sends to me. God may not have anyone else to send to speak life into a situation which is breaking apart a family or a church.*

God has made it clear to me. I'm not here on earth to merely do life my way and according to my plan. That thinking may actually cause me to miss the purpose and plan God has 'in store for me' while I am here on earth.

THE TRUTH: We are Joint Heirs with Christ.

We are to align with God's will and pray God's Kingdom Come and God's Will Be Done. Then, we are to pass our inheritance on to the 3rd and 4th generation, which includes the layers of our family which are present in our lives during our lifetime!

Romans 8: 12-19. Sonship Through the Spirit

Therefore, brethren, we are debtors—not to the flesh, to live according to the flesh. ^{13} For if you live according to the flesh you will die; but if by the Spirit you put to death the deeds of the body, you will live. ^{14} For as many as are led by the Spirit of God, these are sons of God. ^{15} For you did not receive the spirit of bondage again to fear, but you received the Spirit of adoption by whom we cry out, "Abba, Father." ^{16} The Spirit Himself bears witness with our spirit that we are children of God, ^{17} and if children, then heirs —heirs of God and joint heirs with Christ, if indeed we suffer with *Him,* that we may also be glorified together. **From Suffering to Glory.** ^{18} For I consider that the sufferings of this present time are not worthy *to be compared* with the glory which shall be revealed in us. ^{19} For the earnest expectation of the creation eagerly waits for the revealing of the sons of God.

God's Currency

God's plan is based upon living our life according to God's currency for everything and we are not able to do that until we are functioning within ***God's Storehouse Principle.***

God's currency is not the process of going from buying to bartering. God's currency is exchanging all that we have and all that we are with others in the body of Christ so all are blessed and none leave the assembly or have to live their life in lack, in need. **Example:** God introduced me to a widow. She was left with a substantial monthly income in addition to a huge estate. She felt she needed to give more and more and more to the church. After giving a tithe of the estate, she gave a $35,000 grand piano to the church in her husband's memory as she loved piano music. The church sold the piano for about half the amount and used the funds for to pay expenses within their budget. The amount she paid for the piano would have purchased a home and possibly a used auto 'free and clear' for a family in some parts of America. We have to be cautious what we do within God's Storehouse, God's currency!

Many have talked with me at length about comparing us as a body of believers to the church in Ephesus, Corinth and Philippi, etc., however we have not retained the standard of the churches established by the apostles in order for us to be considered as a similar structure let alone a people living in a fashion which is even close to the same as the church of the Ephesians, or the Corinthians, or the Philippians.

They gathered together as the entire community of believers in Christ and they proceeded per the structure of the apostles, as you see per Paul's letters. Encouragement shared. Confirmations stated by the people regarding holding each other accountable and responsible to hold the standard set. Sharing the words God sends through the prophets which confirm the word, the truth. Reminders to keep the people aligned with God's will and to conform our mind and heart to Christ, keeping Christ foremost in our thoughts, plans and actions as Christ is the Chief Cornerstone, the head of the Church.

The apostles and prophets traveled church to church sharing the testimonies and blessings with the people while keeping the people focused on the needs of all in the community who gathered together in the assembly and those beyond the walls so none shall live in their community or leave their gathering in lack. That structure is the same for the church today. Sadly, it is not the focus or the plan of the church today.

God Revealed the Truth in Bite Sized Pieces

God's Storehouse Principle became the theme as I was asked to preach in churches around the world. I'm not an ordained or 'papered' pastor. God orchestrated the extensive travel church to church, business to business and nation to nation after preparing me enough to get out of the whale Jonah as found himself in so I could experience living in awe and wonder each step of the way.

Since God started with a card-carrying, pew-warming, protestant denominational gal at a point in time when I could do nothing in the world, there was a lot of preparation which needed to take place! ***It's A Faith Walk!*** includes a few of the details regarding about seven months of a three year journey. God revealed a lot to me each and every day.

God proved the scriptures as His training took place prior to being sent to each region and His depth of training did not stop when God orchestrated global travel since I was sent 'without an extra coin or tunic' where He set me before Governors and Kings, arranged personal introductions before I arrived and confirmed plans after I showed up since God was 'filling me as an empty vessel' with the exact words precisely when they were needed.

Like many who have asked me about the signs and wonders, I wanted to see the signs, wonders and miracles, also. I did not realize it was my limited human understanding (church & Christian education training) which was blocking the experience.

God had to re-define nearly everything!

God pointed out where the lies of the enemy have affected us in every aspect of our daily life and He confirmed this was always the plan of the enemy, to tempt us to choose the world view and miss what God has 'in store' for us!

- # 1 Time. Spending more time with God changes everything!
- # 2 Cash flow and pay off vs. increasing credit which is really debt, causing us to become deeply indebted!
- # 3 Planning, which results in accomplishing much.
- # 4 Sharing Talents, Skills and Abilities to bless.
- # 5 Realizing who the People are in our Network, ensuring our Inner Circle people inspire and encourage us, and support our dreams; sharing Resources to fulfill upon the plans God reveals.
- # 6 Confirming balance in our personal life, first, then, in our business life, and then, with all of our life in focus, living fully balanced in our life!
- # 7 Discipling others and taking on new assignments as we grow and mature in all God has 'in store' for us, living blessed and sharing the blessings, truth, wisdom and word

of knowledge with all who have ears to hear and eyes to see God's truth.

Gaining the same understanding so we can live in harmony, expressing and living in the peace of Christ which is a peace that God provides and it surpasses all human understanding.

Philippians 2: 2-4. Unity Through Humility

Therefore if *there is* any consolation in Christ, if any comfort of love, if any fellowship of the Spirit, if any affection and mercy, 2 fulfill my joy by being like-minded, having the same love, *being* of one accord, of one mind. 3 *Let* nothing *be done* through selfish ambition or conceit, but in lowliness of mind let each esteem others better than himself. 4 Let each of you look out not only for his own interests, but also for the interests of others.

Unite Us Lord as One Body, operating in One Accord! Once we gain understanding, a key issue we need to address is: Discipleship. Why? It is missing. Without discipleship, the body of Christ remains in the infant stage unable to walk in faith, let alone power and authority.

We are to sharpen each other as iron sharpens iron.

Proverbs 27:17

As iron sharpens iron, so a man sharpens the countenance of his friend.

May it become for us as it Paul was with the Ephesians.

Ephesians 1: 15-23. Prayer for Spiritual Wisdom

Therefore I also, after I heard of your faith in the Lord Jesus and your love for all the saints, [16] do not cease to give thanks for you, making mention of you in my prayers: [17] that <u>the God of our Lord Jesus Christ</u>, the <u>Father of glory</u>, may give to you <u>the spirit of wisdom and revelation in the knowledge of Him</u>, [18] the <u>eyes of your understanding</u> being enlightened; that <u>you may know what is the hope of His calling, what are the riches of the glory of His inheritance</u> in the saints, [19] and <u>what *is* the exceeding greatness of His power toward us who believe, according to the working of His mighty power</u> [20] which He worked in Christ when He raised Him from the dead and seated *Him* at His right hand in the heavenly *places,* [21] <u>far above all principality and power and might and dominion</u>, and every name that is named, not only in this age but also in that which is to come. [22] <u>And He put all *things* under His feet, and gave Him *to be* head over all *things* to the church,</u> [23] <u>which is His body, the fullness of Him who fills all in all</u>.

Chapter 3 God's Storehouse Principle: Blessings

Will We Become an Empty Vessel, to Become Formed and Filled With Truth & Faith?

Time for a Reality Check

Our human mind thinks small so it causes us to operate small. To understand ***God's Storehouse Principle*** we need to change our perspective for God's plans are BIG!

1 Corinthians 2:9

"Eye has not seen, nor ear heard, nor have entered into the heart of man, the things which God has ('in store') prepared for those who love Him." (NIV) *"No eye has seen, no ear has heard, no mind has conceived what God has ('in store') prepared for those who love him"*

God's Storehouse, Filled to the Rafters

I heard a story, a testimony about *God's Storehouse Principle.* A man was in surgery when he was taken to heaven. God showed him a huge warehouse.

When they entered, together, the man saw miles of gifts all wrapped in white glossy paper and tied with beautiful red bows.

The packages were stacked neatly and identified with our names on each tag. God directed the man to his specific stack. It was so high the man could not see the top of the stack. He was in shock.

God explained that most of the gifts we possess since birth, our talents, skills and abilities and resources gained over time, things which could help others, the blessings God has prepared for us to receive and to share, often remain in the stack during our lifetime.

We do not understand the process of what we are to do when two or more gather together for we do not realize the power available with Christ in the midst because we are fellowshipping with each other.

We are to be about our Father's Kingdom business, exactly as Christ was, sharing the blessings we are and all of what we have with each other so none shall leave the assembly or live in lack.

Pew warming, seeking a good word once a weekd should not be enough for us, for Christ resides in our heart and we are to operate in power and authority so all shall be blessed and none leave the assembly or live in lack.

God confirmed some believers only believe part of the truth and portions of God's word. Many believe Pentecost happened. Many believe key parts of God's word or most of it. However, there are many who do not believe that we are empowered by the Holy Spirit with gifts to walk in power and authority so we can do all God has need of us to do while we are here on earth. Sad but true, many in the church have aligned with the world and believe the only apostles were the only original twelve with Christ.

Jesus taught to us pray the Lord's prayer: ***"(His) kingdom come, (His) will be done (so it shall be) on earth as it is in heaven..."***

When we are not functioning as the true church with the apostles and prophets or walking in power and authority guided by the Holy Spirit, we can be very close to (standing next to) and yet miss God!

We will not realize the truth of how God will replace, restore and bless beyond all that we can pray for or do when He is able to guide us step by step with each other so His work will be done.

White boxes with red bows. Gifts unopened and people in need.

That is a visual that is imprinted in my mind.

It shifted my thinking. I realized 'my good deeds' cannot out do God. When I heard this, I remembered people quoting God is a BIG God and wants to bless, but, in all of my years in church, I was not seeing the blessings flow as the Doxology states: *"Praise God from whom all blessings flow..."*

I dismissed the thought since I had experienced some devastating, life-altering circumstances and the church supported the fact I need to get it back on the right track and then I will be blessed. But, the experiences were so severe they separated me from people in the church over time because they wanted to see it 'get better'. They actually said: *"Bad things do not happen to good people"* ... *"You must have done something to upset God."*

The negative experiences and the negative comments from 'well meaning' people in the church both rendered me speechless.

Then, God provided some relief from the 'well meaning' people when I called a dear prayer partner and she told me, *"If you could run into the street and throw out your top three problems, would you do it?"* The answer took no time to calculate for it would be great to be able to merely throw away my problems.

But then, she said, *"Now, since all of your neighbors had the same offer and they did the same thing, which ones would you run out and pick up if you knew everybody was going to run out and pick up three?"*

Wow, I was shocked. That did not take time to calculate, either, since I am comfortable with the problems I am dealing with. However, she said, *"Why are you holding on to any problems? Do you believe God will guide you through any problem you might experience or not?"*

I was so used to carrying everything, holding on to everything, I was stuck in my own mess and most of it was my own making. Then I heard the cliche comment: *"Let go and Let God!"* Simple. Specific. It was a wake-up call!

God Cares So Deeply; Sometimes He Reminds Us

God delivered a word through a woman attending a conference. I told the people who said I must have upset God that God and I are fine but there are some unsavory people ... but, perhaps I did not take it in that God would deeply feel the experience I was going through until I heard her say: *God showed me a vision of a courtroom. God told me that he wants you to know that He was with you when you experienced a tragic judgment in the courtroom. God told me it was so severe, God wants you to know that even He cried.* This was a new revelation for me, to think that God saw me in the depth of my pain, a court matter which was so severe even He cried.

Christian Music Which Speaks To Us

A special song which has meant a lot in the low moments while grasping the truth vs. what I have heard for so many years is *Who Am I* by Casting Crowns and a good follow-up is their song: *Praise You In The Storm,* followed by *Voice of Truth* and *Courageous.* All available on You Tube.

Lord, may we release all, repent of all, request forgiveness of all and then help us forgive ourselves of all so we will live free and be able to proceed as empty vessels to be filled with Your wisdom and knowledge so we accomplish more than we could possibly imagine in our lifetime 'as a human!'

Psalms 22:3-5.

… You *are* holy, enthroned in the praises of Israel. [4] Our fathers trusted in You; They trusted, and You delivered them. [5] They cried to You, and were delivered; They trusted in You, and were not ashamed.

May we come together and fellowship, hear the needs of the people and tithe from all that we are and have 'in this world.'

Matthew 18:20.

For where two or three are gathered together in My name, I am there in the midst of them."

An Empty Vessel

I trust it will not be as difficult for you as it was for me to become an 'empty vessel' so God could fill me with His word, His wisdom for the situation exactly in the moment when it is needed.

It makes me think about the study I did in genealogy to trace our family lines back to Norway, England and Scotland. Our English ancestors were Church of England (Episcopalian), Scottish relatives were Church of Scotland (Presbyterian), and Norwegian relatives were Scandinavian Lutheran. In the Scotland to Canada to

America research, I found an obituary of a great-great aunt whose husband stated she was many wonderful things and then he added 'of Quaker ancestors.' This was a shock!

They came to America for religious and financial freedom. I learned about the separation of church and state from them, as they did not want a Church of America!

Since nothing in the family bibles indicated a relative was linked to Quakers, I called to check with my Mom. Dad answered the call and set the record straight with his response, ***"There's nobody in your Mom's family quiet enough to be a Quaker!"***

As you can tell from my Dad's confirmation, God had a lot to do to help me completely empty this vessel for God to be able to fill me to overflowing. It's the more of God / Holy Spirit and less of me / flesh process. It is a blessing because you will only want God's truth and wisdom to be expressed to the people. It is critical to seek the Lord's training and the Holy Spirit's infilling so we can proceed with the step-by-step guidance as you will see when you read the adventurous day when the witches danced and attempted to poison me in Africa and then the night when a voodoo princess tried to curse me off the planet during a Spiritual Warfare Conference in Earl's Court, London!

When empty and fully submitted, God can do mighty things and all that is needed will be provided.

God Arranged Two Phone Lines
After the World Confirmed: No Way!

One of the most unique provision moments. Due to the severe circumstances (judges and an attorney were sentenced to prison on Federal RICO charges), I was placed on multiple Social Security and Driver's License Numbers and it was supposedly required to keep me on a protected record. That was not the truth. The truth was different, my record was merged together the entire time. The devastation was extensive. I was done re-starting my life without a work or credit history. I did not take one step to re-establish my life for three years. I did not set up a phone, purchase an auto, or establish a bank or credit account. I told God I could do nothing!

This is when God took me by the hand and arranged all details for global travel. All provision was handled without making a request and autos were arranged when needed.

Then, there was a man God spoke to. He insisted that I needed to have two phone lines installed in my home: A major testimony is based upon a man from New Zealand who was doing business in London ignoring 'the facts' as I knew 'the facts' from experience. A new 'God lesson' for me!

He found my 'no phone or fax line' status to be unacceptable as a Business Coach. He said, *"I need to be able to call you and FAX information to you so when you return to America set up two phone lines."*

I explained why this was not possible, but, he said, *"...if you have to, set them up in my name and if the phone company wants to check on my record you can tell them I am with AT&T."* Even with AT&T this seemed impossible.

When I called the top manager of the local phone company she said exactly what I knew she would say because the company would not be able to issue phone lines due to starting over with a new record but refusing to change my name or move out of the area. The phone company had merged the record and they knew multiple social security numbers were issued to me and that was not 'feasible' to the staff so I was denied.

I waited a few moments before I called the phone company again. This time, I said I was setting up the lines for the man and I only confirmed his details: **1.** a citizen of New Zealand, **2.** working in England, and **3.** needing two phone lines. This time, the manager did not ask if the man had any form of ID to confirm he existed, or if he had a phone record with AT&T. She only wanted to know his social security number. When I reminded her he was born in New Zealand so he does not have a social security number, without hesitation she asked, ***"Ah, that's right. Does he want a morning or afternoon appointment tomorrow?"***

As a citizen, the wait would be about 10-14 days. However, without knowing anything about the man or that he even exists, the phone lines were established the next day.

Since that day, it has been impossible to change the lines back to my name even though I am the one paying the monthly bills. So, 'on paper' the two phone lines had to remain in his name.

God orchestrates a solution and fulfills a specific need within a moment when we live aligned with ***God's Storehouse Principle.***

The man was a man of God. He found my situation to be unacceptable. He offered to step in while he had no requirement 'in the world' to ensure that I would be able to set up phone lines in America. Without hesitation, he stepped up, offered to help and even have the bill sent to him if that would resolve the problem.

Alone, I had no answer for this problem. *Lord, help us hear Your voice so we know how to fulfill upon the needs of Your lambs.*

Are we doing what we can to care for the widows (the world has so impacted the group that God includes all without husbands)? Are we caring for the orphans (the world has so impacted the group that God includes all without fathers)? When God looks upon us, does he see people standing firm in faith? So firm, before we even put on the armor?

Company Closed

Out of Time to Search before Departing Flight

God arranged for me to be in a different part of the world within 24 hours of a return flight. I needed a something which I had only found at a specific store. I scheduled the day within the tight time frame available. When I arrived at the store, the notice on the front of the building confirmed the company had closed all of their stores during the days while God had extended me for seven weeks in another nation. In that moment, as the tears welled up in my eyes because I needed every spare moment to drive to this store location and make one more stop to return the renatal car. I was upset. God merely smiled and gently told me to go ahead and drive to the drugstore.

I laughed. This is not a product which is available at the local drugstore. However, God was insistent and I only had enough time to stop at the local drugstore on my way home. I had to finish packing (a few items were still in the clothes dryer when I left the house due to the short turn around time) and then I had to immediately go to the airport.

As I entered the store, I asked a young man if he could help me find the product. He was excited because he stocked the shelves with this new product the night before. The new manager just moved to the area. His wife had not lived near the beach before. She wanted him to supply the product and that is how God orchestrated provision of my need before it was required!

The only other stop, to return the rental car, resulted in receiving new information the LORD was aware of when He rescheduled the last moments before the flight. Plus, the LORD saved me the expense of taking the shuttle to the airport. I always dropped the rental car off and took the shuttle to the airport. However, the LORD helped me remove that expense by informing me I could drop off the car at the airport. The rental car company confirmed and I was at the airport in time for the international departure.

Grow In Faith!

Faith Made Evident

When God arranged for me to be in Ghana, West Africa, I attended a church service with Pastor Sam Ankrah due to God orchestrating a ride from the hotel with a man who did not know me, yet, Pastor Charles Benneh. God told me the exact moment to go to the lobby and who to ask for a ride to church. God's provision led to a friendship which included attendance at a church in Ghana and for Pastor Charles' ordination in London with the opportunity to meet his wife and son; a friendship to this day.

God showed me so much within minutes. I was amazed and in awe of the faith expressed by the people. It was in early August. The heat and humidity were both about 100. The men were in long sleeve shirts and ties, holding white kerchiefs while dancing and praising the Lord. Their faces were radiant. Their smiles were contagious. This was a new type of 'church experience', clearly not 'an American church experience'. I've not seen men dancing as though nobody is watching, and praising let alone doing it in the extreme hot temperature with high humidity.

I asked Pastor Sam and he said, *"They are like you. They live by faith, but, it is different for the people here, as they have to pay at least $200/month in rent alone and most of the people do not earn $200/month. Their testimonies are strong for you see they have to depend upon God's provision in their life every day of their life."*

I felt I was filled with faith and I knew my life was spirit filled, while the training program with God is like 'on the job training' as we continue to learn how to live by God's word and proceed per the guidance of the Holy Spirit. LORD reign!

NOTE: Faith Monument and details on pages 221-222.

Chapter 4 God's Storehouse Principle: Perspective

Our Human Perspective Has to Change!
We Remember What We Are Told and
What We Are Told / Believe, Forms Our Perspective

When I was invited to Shanghai, China, the first meetings were held in the Bank of China building in the world famous area known as the Pudong. I had just arrived in China. I was excited beyond belief.

As I entered the building, the receptionist asked a few questions about my personal needs for the meeting, i.e., water, coffee or tea, etc.

Then, the first sentences of her conversation were for my information. She wanted to be sure I knew about the invasion and occupation of China by the Japanese. I was shocked. She seemed quite upset. I wondered how I had missed a critical, global news event. My mind was scrolling through the many news stories while I was thinking I must have missed the announcement of this global event either while I was in Kuala Lumpur, Malaysia (during Ramadan no less; ah, God's sense of humor!) the prior week or during my flight from Malaysia to China the day before.

It was an interesting first statement for a new conversation. Before I could take it in, the factual declaration of war and occupation of the country, it was a fact that was immediately confirmed by the assistant to the President upon meeting her. As soon as she opened the door to the executive suite, she handed me a bottle of chilled water and repeated the exact same facts with the exact same level of concern while I waited to meet with the President. The receptionist may have been 19 or 20 years old. The assistant to the President is a recent graduate of the University, so she was probably 22 or 23 years old.

When I met with the bank President, I asked him if there was a huge global event I was not aware of due to hearing very little news the past two weeks while I was traveling. He seemed concerned and wanted to know what type of event I was referring to, so I told him I was concerned about the potential of China's pending war with Japan. He laughed. He was surprised I was not aware of the invasion of China, Manchuria, by Japan which took place in 1931 or that the occupation continued until the end of the eight year war from 1937 until 1945. He said the women were very glad American troops helped after the bombing of Pearl Harbor as the Americans helped China bring the China-Japan war to an end and he trusted they wanted me, as an American, to know they are grateful.

Clearly, this 'event' took place many decades prior to the birth of the receptionist or the assistant, even before the birth of the President. However, it is a key fact the children learn in school. They wanted me to know this as it is ingrained within their culture that the Chinese people will not be occupied again. Nobody was able to 'Google' and find out that Japan was a small island nation with a much smaller population. As the body of Christ, even though we can Google to find out the facts, we have always had the truth 'in hand' but we need to re-check what we heard with God's word and know what we are hearing is truth! LORD reign!

Perspective, learned: I have a good example to show how slight compromises with the world have caused us to appear to be more like the world than the body of Christ. If I invited you for tea and I told you we were going to meet at the pagoda you would want to know about the location. So, let's say I send you a photo and ask you to meet me at this one?

If you have not visited China, you may not realize that one of the biggest differences in China is that the sky is always gray.

A glare makes it appear light gray. Almost no blue sky is visible in the sky and there are no clouds.

It is a different experience. The gray sky provides a very different background!

In this example, let's say that at about the exact same time I extend my invitation to you another friend sends you an invitation with a photo inserted and they make it appear to be an official invitation with date, time, address, etc

Would you prefer to meet with me or would you prefer to meet or would you prefer to meet your other friend at this location?

The pagoda is the exact same structure. The photos are the exact same size, but the second photo has a nice border and looks more professional.

The second photo was cropped so it appears the photographer has zoomed in to be closer to the Pagoda. This view also improves upon the original photo by adding amazing clouds and color which make the gardens look great. It significantly changes the 'perspective' of the scene.

So, are you thinking that a get together at the 2nd pagoda would be better? Survey says: Most Christians are making decisions based upon how a person looks, how a ministry looks or sounds or aligns with their own personal desires and thoughts vs looking for confirmation in scripture and the fruit of the ministry!

A better checklist: Is the glory of God evident? Is the fellowship bible based and Spirit-filled?

The photo with the gray sky is the original, real photo.

The second photo is a photo shop version. It also includes a Hawaiian sky. The changes were done by a fellow instructor within the Buckminster Fuller Business School for Entrepreneurs program while we were in Shenzhen, China. He took the original photograph. Since it seemed dull to him, he cropped the photo and added the special border. Then, he enhanced the photo due to being from Hawaii by adding a Hawaiian sky.

Insignificant details at first glance?

Not so insignificant when it causes us to actually choose a counterfeit!

The changes:

1. closer to the pagoda,

2. border added,
3. Hawaiian sky,

Subtle changes however, this is what a 'close counterfeit' looks like.

Because we want to be comfortable, politically correct and respectful of all of the input from the world, we forget this is how the devil tempts us, lures us away from God's invitation and plans 'in store' which He has prepared for us!

The subtle differences are what the devil uses in an effort to tempt or trap us. This is like the TV commercial question:

1. Got God?
2. Got the Counterfeit? Compromised with the devil?

Why is Perspective So Important?

God's plan, ***God's Storehouse Principle,*** is clear. Adjusting the plan over time by 'humanizing' the process causes the plan to be a world plan which no longer resembles God's plan. We are not to lean on our own / world understanding. We are to live per the word and guidance of the Holy Spirit.

Proverbs 3:4-6

And so find favor and high esteem in the sight of God and man. [5] Trust in the Lord with all your heart, And lean not on your own understanding; [6] In all your ways acknowledge Him, And He shall direct your paths.

Within *It's A Faith Walk!* I shared what God showed me within a series of visions within one night to wake me up!

Three Visions

During the night, God showed me three visions. Within the first one I was surrounded by all of my 'projects', courses I taught at the University for a new Management Certificate Program, conference speaking topics, Entrepreneurial course materials for the US Federal contracts, etc., topics on top confirmed the stacks were representative of the entire accomplishments in my life to date, so there were stacks of paper everywhere as a fairly large funnel appeared. I was staring at the bottom of the funnel to see exactly what God was going to show me, as God scooped up all of the papers and inserted them into the funnel. But, as soon as the funnel was filled with all of my stuff, God merely tapped the small end of the funnel.

All of the papers fell in all directions. As I watched them flying through the air no specific items were being identified. I did not realize God had put his hand through the small end of the funnel until I saw God pull me through. It was a shock to watch the movie of my life with God picking me up. All God had in his hand, was me. I was so human in that moment, plus I was confused because not one topic appeared amongst the papers so I asked, *"What do you want from me?"* And the Holy Spirit softly confirmed when I saw God's hand lift me up higher in the air, *"What I want is you."*

It was a humbling experience. I had no idea what God could do with me. I was in tears as God began to show me the second vision. I was on a platform with the floodlights on the stage shining bright. God made it a familiar experience as it was exactly what I experience as a conference speaker. It was exciting because I recognized all of the people in the first rows. God said, *"You are here for them."* I told God it was not very much to fill my life, by being here for the people I already know. As I said this, God turned the floodlights on the multitude and it stretched out across the land in all directions. I immediately confirmed I did not know any of these people as God stated, *"Because you blessed the ones you know, they blessed the rest."*

I was embarrassed. To me, this sounded rather lofty. God knew my concern, so he showed me the third vision. God turned the view to show me a profile view of me so I could see the words leaving my lips and going out to the front rows and then bouncing throughout the multitude. I was in awe as God showed me how His words leave my mouth and they travel to the heart of the first person and on to the next and the next, on and on until they reach the multitude. It appeared the same to me as a stone does when it is cast upon the water and it touches the water many times while it skips across a lake. God knew I used to try and make stones skip across the water with cousins when I was young so God used that analogy and it made sense to me. However, I still felt as though I was incapable of being a representative for God, an Ambassador for Christ.

Confessions of a non-Bible Scholar. As I shared this fact with the Honorable Minister of Finance in Tonga, Tasi, after he shared his multiple degrees from top universities plus his bible scholar background, I could only confirm I have some degrees but, I am not a bible scholar and I believe God orchestrated my travel to be in the Kingdom of Tonga to serve. He cried and God smiled.

When I confirmed to God what He already knew, I am not a bible scholar, God reminded me that He orchestrated all details and breathed the life into the powerful men of God who spoke God's truth within the Bible. They did not memorize the bible prior to their journey. God confirmed the truth: He walked with them and He walks with us. His scriptures are provided by Him through the Holy Spirit in the exact moment they are needed. Within a few months of my journey, a pastor friend told the people to watch me when I speak as I do not need notes. If I need a fact, God provides it. Plus, He includes the scripture reference! Grateful to serve.

Lord Help Us Fulfill Upon Your Vision For Our Life!

Have you seen the Disney movie *The Kid* starring Bruce Willis? Synopsis: *An unhappy and disliked image consultant gets a second shot at life when an eight year old version of himself mysteriously appears.* It is so good, every client was required to view it with their family! Two clients returned to see it together after seeing it with their family. Amazing reports because the 'turning 40' version thinks he has a great life but, he is in shock and unable to speak when he realizes the kid is absolutely him at eight years old. The kid <u>easily</u> confirms his life does not look good! With the fancy home and over 200 TV channels, there is nothing to watch and, all of his dreams about who he wants to be by the time he is 40, aka old, have not turned out as he had hoped: **No wife, no kids and no dog!**

Are you still 'on course' with the dreams and visions the LORD has given to you or have you settled? May your prayer request include asking God to open the eyes of your heart to see His vision of who you are through His eyes. May each day from this day forward become aligned with God's will and God's BIG plans for you to have a great, fulfilled Kingdom life!

Chapter 5 God's Storehouse Principle: Wake-up Call!

My Personal Perspective Had To Change

God Showed Me Why Our Perspective Has To Change

God arranged for me to journey with Him around the globe. *It's A Faith Walk!* includes a few of th especifics regarding how God had to work with me and have God sized patience with me so I could clearly understand His plan vs the world based plan.

God showed me a lot about us as humans and what we have learned within and from the church, the structure, and how limited and 'off base' my (our) human perspective has become over time.

Personally, I only knew what I had heard from my Lutheran perspective and it was confirmed within what I was taught at Augustana Lutheran College. Then, I was challenged when I attended Pepperdine University a school within the Churches of

Christ denomination which was the church affiliation of the Founder and contributor of the entire parcel of land granted to the University in Malibu, California by George Pepperdine.

California also presented a challenge since I grew up in a community where the Scandinavians were Lutheran and the Germans were Catholic. In California, I quickly met a lot of Scandinavians who were Catholic and Germans who were Lutheran. LORD reign!

I only had a Lutheran perspective prior to attending Pepperdine University. So, 100% of my understanding and knowledge and all prior Christian conversations were based upon what I learned while attending the Scandinavian Lutheran church and college. I did not know the perspective of the 65 divisions or synods merged together within the Evangelical Lutheran Church of America.

Before, during and after Pepperdine, I did not attend a service for the Churches of Christ. I only knew they were established to become the church of the New Testament, and their goal was to unite together the believers who wanted to come together and live per the Bible. That seemed to align with my training.

However, I did not know that they had a significant split in their church due to people not wanting musical instruments to be involved in worship. They also had two arguments which caused problems: **1.** no organizational structure above the congregational level, and **2.** the theological approach to the interpretation of the Bible.

Our perspective is not always based upon the truth in the Holy Bible if we focus only upon parts of scripture and no administration or organizational structure above the congregation or fellowship is right per the scriptures.

During flight layover times in nations where people cannot afford for me to come but they want me to preach to their gathering or denomination, they are grateful I will meet with them until I hear the restrictions: **1.** I cannot arrive 'in make-up' for their denomination does not allow make-up to be worn, **2.** All of my hair has to be piled on top of my head because it is a woman's crown and I had no way to obtain clips to work with the hair (it is full, wavy, curly and many other exciting things, but is not the type of hair that is easily gathered together and piled on top of the head), **3.** They do not allow women to wear pants and I typically travel in a pants outfit, **4.** They want me to share the amazing things God is doing but NOT mention the Holy Spirit. So sad because if I cannot bring the Holy Spirit with me, then I have nothing to say.

What have I learned about all of this by taking it to our LORD? I do know that He cries with us! *LORD forgive us!*

I can testify to the goodness of God for the people who were not accepting of these 'issues' for our LORD shows up in the gathering of believers and the people quickly forget their important requirements the moment God shows up mightily and the glory of God fills the gathering and all in the assembly are blessed beyond measure. Those who receive the blessings are the ones who have ears to hear and eyes to see the glory of the LORD. They can let go of human judgments and fellowship with the believers.

Sometimes we just have to get over some hurdles aka man made judgments, the things we make important when we do not leave the judgments up to God and seek what our God is doing in the people we gather together with. ***LORD help us see people through your eyes!***

May we let our LORD show up mightily when two or more gather together for we cannot do or predict or try and outdo anything He can do within a life in moment of time.

What Happened?

Often, without even realizing it, we believe and then follow a 'speaker', a 'pastor' or a 'leader' who shares facts that make logical or worldly sense. So, we feel we can accept their perspective. What? We would need to question ourselves at this point because this is the process of leaning upon our own human understanding and a world based structure.

We may make a personal choice to follow that person because 'it sounds good'. We may get involved with that man or ministry without seeking the full truth and knowing that we know the information being shared is the truth, the whole truth, and nothing but the truth so help me God!

Emphasis on the ***help me God*** part!

Matthew 28:18-20

And Jesus came and spoke to them, saying, "All authority has been given to Me in heaven and on earth. [19] Go therefore and make disciples of all the nations, baptizing them in the name of the Father and of the Son and of the Holy Spirit, [20] teaching them to observe all things that I have commanded you; and lo, I am with you always, even to the end of the age." Amen.

Verse 19 is critical. God does not say go forth and make some to be ___ (insert the title of any denomination) and some to be ___ (you get the idea). God does not say go forth and 'convert', only to disciple and to those who have ears to hear and eyes to see. Instead of uniting together as fellow believers, one body of Christ gathering together all Christians, some Christians became Independents or Separatists or Congregationalists, or another group.

Some followed Wesley and became Methodists. Some lived in England and therefore they were part of the government church, Church of England, which changed back and forth from Roman Catholic to Anglican or Episcopalian, based upon the belief of the Monarch. Some lived in Scotland and became Presbyterians which was the government church or Church of Scotland. God made it clear. We were not to follow any man's perspective. We are not to lean on our own or man's understanding.

Proverbs 3:4-6.

And so find favor and high esteem in the sight of God and man. [5] <u>Trust in the Lord with all your heart, And lean not on your own</u>

understanding; ⁶ In all your ways acknowledge Him, And He shall direct your paths.

But, that is what former generations did and that is what we do. We follow man so long as they align with our thinking.

Not only does the enemy isolate us, we isolate ourselves from the body of Christ based upon what we think we know or what we believe or what we think sounds good to us, but we have to be careful we are not leaning on our own understanding and living separate from God's word.

As soon as we think the ministry does not align with what sounds good to us we decide to move to a different church led by a different man with a way of thinking that does align.

This is human. This is how the denominations began.

When Jesus directed us to go forth and disciple, he meant to draw the people to Him, to the Father and do as the Father does and honor the commandments, discipling as we journey through our life, equipping and training others.

Instead of discipling into the fellowship of believers, the process became human guiding vs. Holy Spirit guiding and that is how we ended up with so many denominations.

In each 'denomination,' a man established the basis of 'thinking' which led to the foundation of the denomination.

An Example: Since I was raised Lutheran and I know the denomination was started on October 31 (we did not celebrate Halloween, we met at the church and colored Lutheran emblems and received candy), I will start with the Lutheran denomination. Martin Luther hung his 95 theses on the Castle Church door in Wittinberg in 1517. Martin Luther was a priest in the Roman Catholic church prior to posting the theses.

Another Example: The Anglican (England) & Episcopalian churches stem from the Church of England, when there was no separation of church and state and the church was a government church. The Church of England was established by King Henry VIII when he had to break away from Pope and the requirements of the Catholic church after he was excommunicated for his divorce from his wife Catherine of Aragon. He made himself the head of the church, making the Anglican church (Church of England) the official government church. Then, he was free per his new rules and available to marry Ann Boleyn. Later, his daughter Queen Mary I (raised Roman Catholic) returned the structure to the Roman Catholic church with the Pope as the Supreme head of the church. Soon after, Queen Elizabeth I (raised Protestant) returned the country to the Act of Supremacy & the church to an Anglican government church. She changed the wording of Supreme Head to Supreme Governor, a move to be more inclusive of the Roman Catholic church.

Another Example: The Presbyterian Church stems from the Church of Scotland, when there was no separation of church and state and the church was a government church. The French reformer John Calvin is credited with the foundation of the Presbyterian church.

Another Example: The Methodist church began in England in the 1700's based upon the teachings of John Wesley.

Another Example: Assembly of God which credits the Azusa Street Revival and the reformers: Martin Luther, John Wesley and Dwight Moody.

Another Example: Church of God in Christ has become one of the largest Pentecostal churches in America. The church also credits Azusa Street Revival and the leadership of Elder C H Mason, later becoming Bishop Mason.

Another Example, perhaps the most diverse group: The Baptist church began with the leadership of an English Separatist John Smyth as the Pastor. More than 100 million Baptists worldwide, 33 million in America with the largest group being the Southern Baptist Convention with 16 million members.

Another Example, more neutral: The Congregational church foundation was based upon merely congregations of believers meeting independently in various locations. So, it was perhaps the closest resemblance to the body of Christ, gathering of believers. However, the roots are based upon the theory of union as published by the theologian Robert Browne in 1592. For many, many decades they remained separate and independent, however, they have formed into a typical denomination and there have been splits, since. In fact, in America they have three groups: **1.** United Church of Christ (the largest), **2.** National Association of Congregational Christian Churches, and **3.** Conservative Congregational Christian Conference.

The list goes on and on and on and on and on and on. **The key point is:** the only supreme leader of the church is God the Father. The only Savior and Cornerstone is Jesus Christ. When we fellowship together, two or more, Christ is in the midst. The only guide though all of this is the Holy Spirit.

Fellow believers, we have work to do!

And, we can do better!

A very special church identified within *It's A Faith Walk!*, Pastor Steve Dittmar, Jubilee Church in Camarillo. I've been richly blessed each time I share time with the fellowship. They were prompted to bless the widows. God confirmed seven widows would be blessed at $3,000 each. The church prepared everything in advance with the bank for the crisp, new $100 bills to be available. God sent seven widows and the church shared $21,000 with them. During another service, Pastor Steve confirmed the church has enough to meet all of the needs and they also provide a food pantry, resources and services, etc., for those in need, and 24/7 prayer coverage with teams of three praying in the church every three hours, etc., so he said the people were to seek who the Holy Spirit prompts them to bless and what they are to do to bless them. Many men ran to get something for water to wash the feet of their wives. Some shared cash, services or words of blessing. Many were blessed within fifteen minutes of time!

God's Message

During *It's A Faith Walk!* God gave me a very clear message about the status of the church, the body of Christ: "***Not enough of*** *my men are preparing and putting on their steel toed boots to march with Me, so I am having to call forth My women, even My widows and My orphans, to prepare My Army to march with Me before the SONrise."*

I had no idea what God meant by steel toed boots, however, I was quickly informed by living in a military town that every person serving in the military knows this is 'required issue' as part of their uniform before they go into battle.

Fellow believers, we have a lot of work to do to right the wrongs!

To accomplish all that is required we have to shift 180 degrees away from all of the world based thoughts and plans we have heard and followed up to this point in time and learn God's truth so we can fulfill upon our purpose; focus 100% on God's plans to function within ***God's Storehouse Principle.***

Can The Church, The Body Of Christ Grow to Adulthood?

I am constantly asked if it is possible.

May I have a drum roll, please?

The answer is: With God and His wisdom, it is possible.

God's plan is and always was simple and clear.

God's word and His desire is to guide us through the Holy Spirit each step of the way.

God's Plan: Pure Religion
James 1:27

Pure and undefiled religion ... **to visit orphans and widows in their trouble,** *and* **to keep oneself unspotted from the world.**

John 21:15

[*Jesus Restores Peter*] So when they had eaten breakfast, Jesus said to Simon Peter, *"Simon, son of Jonah, do you love Me more than these?"* He said to Him, *"Yes, Lord; You know that I love You."* He said to (Peter), ***"Feed My lambs."***

So many times I am asked to start an orphanage in a nation while I am there because people will donate a lot of money to me / a ministry if I do that.

God has been clear, he wants us to empty the orphanages into the homes of the believers!

One Sunday I was asked to preach in a church in America (rare, but with God's prompting during meetings with the pastors and their leadership it does happen). I shared a few details with the California church regarding ***God's Storehouse Principle.***

Within 30 days, the pastor contacted me while I was in London. He shared powerful, amazing testimonies.

The people did not know where the orphanages or offices for the foster care system were located the day I preached, but at least 30 families were in the process of adopting children.

The church made a list of "A Tithe of All" with one column being all of the services, talents, skills and abilities available when the people within the congregation would tithe of who they are. Plus, they made a separate list of all of the needs expressed by all of the people within the fellowship, beginning with the widows and all of women without husbands and the children without fathers.

The people were in awe to see God's wisdom when they realized the two lists were a match. People were deeply blessed! The testimonies were shared far and wide resulting in a second service being added on Sunday morning.

PRAY! Separation of Church and State in America

Did you know that due to the British church of our American Forefathers being controlled by the government, the structure to separate church from state was established so we would not have a church that is controlled by the American Government?

Facts are not represented the same today.

Congress printed the first (10,000) bibles to provide one in every church, school and home in America. Refer to: Faith Monument details, page 221 and 222, movie: ***Monumental.***

Lord, give us Your Truth and more time while You help us learn how to shift our thinking back to Your truth.

To grasp the concept of living our life per ***God's Storehouse Principle,*** we need to know who we are and how to expand our time. Everybody has the same 24 hour day. Only God can expand time. We feel more rested and we need less time to sleep when we know the truth! The secret of expanding / storing / tithing time in our life is God!

Chapter 6   God's Storehouse Principle: Expand Time!

God Expands Time

To begin to comprehend how we can shift from man's plan to God's plan, we need to know truth from lies. We have been told many times that the enemy / the world lies, but we have to realize in the very core (our heart, where Christ resides) that only God's word is the truth and the enemy **exists** to steal, kill & destroy, and lie to us!

The world based plans are everywhere and they have influenced every aspect of our daily life. They are the lies.

People constantly state, *"When I have more time I will ..."* or *"If I had more time I would ..."* This is the lie we have accepted and we repeat it almost without thinking about our words!

The devil's joke is being played on us!

The world has played tricks on us from every angle!

The enemy lies so much, we have 'over time' aligned with several of the lies without realizing it, Lies about time have reduced our lives to a very tight calendar!

Take a moment to look at your calendar. Some calendars are eight hours and one day or no days for the weekend, especially the 'quick reference' calendars. Some are twelve hour days and they insert one day for two, half-day weekend schedules. No matter what type of calendar you choose to use, the world has reduced life into that structure and we live the lie when we pack that structure to overflowing.

Lies keep us from seeing our 24/7 life because calendars are not 24/7 calendars.

So, what happens? We live the lie without realizing it.

We live as though the lies are the truth and we pack the calendar, whether it is an 8 or 12 hour calendar.

Then, we rush home to try and squeeze the ounce or two of life we think we have left since we think it is the only time we can have to 'live' and be with our family and the significant people in our life. But, we are so tired due to what we do not realize the world has done to us during our day, we end up wanting time away from people, time to regain peace before we have to crash. Then, it's hard to crash!

Then, we do it all over again. Everything about this is a part of the lie! We have been living this lie vs. the truth which reveals we are not really living!

Example: Typical Conference Moments
Before My Introduction.

"Is it OK to ask a question right now?" a man whispers loudly from the side of the stage, while I stand in the wings, moments before the conference begins.

"Of course, you are why I am here," I respond, while the staff position my headset microphone and the booth tests sound levels, as I watch people enter.

"No way. How can that be true? You did not know I was going to be here."

"I didn't. I don't have to know. God knows and that is all I need to know." Staff are still working on my lapel microphone and doing a sound check.

"God knows? I'm still not sure if I'm going to stay, so, how would God know?" he says in a louder voice, while clearly becoming very annoyed.

"God knows everything before it happens. God knows you may not choose to stay. If you leave, you will miss the secret God wants to reveal to you, today. Can you afford to do that?" Before I can finish, he interrupts, **"Miss it? Miss what? A secret?"**

"God shares secrets with us, when we spend time with God, but, it does not matter how much God may want to give to you, today, you may decide to not find any time for God. It appears you at that critical point - choice."

He interrupts me, again, as I watch for cues from the stage, **"God would care if I'm here or not?"** The lights begin to dim; music volume softens, as participants take their seats.

Looking for the cue from the stage manager, as I answer with a resounding, **"Yes."** His shock is evident, **"Really?"**

"Yes. Really. As God's servant, all I can tell you right now is that God has known your concern about time, while you have been so busy speaking to everyone in your life about never having any time, and always being out of time, and it's clearly been your conversation for a long time, so, I trust this is why God prompted you to be here, today. It's time for you to hear God's secret."

"Well then, you probably know I have another concern," the man says as he walks even closer, **"I want you to promise me you are not going to be talking about time management. I get so sick of time management seminars."**

"OK, I can absolutely promise you that I'm not going to be talking about time management. Until you know how to expand time, you have no time to manage, anyway ..." as the sound assistant tries to find a good location to run the microphone cord under my suit jacket.

The man continues his objection, while loudly whispering in my ear, being diligent about expressing each word while standing very close to me. So, security approaches while he states, **"I don't need one more person telling me how I should spend my time or manage my time."**

"You sound convinced. Now, I'm convinced...you have no time to have a life," I respond, while I waive off the security guards.

"Good!" But then, as he turns away he realizes what I said and he turns back on his heels. *"What?"*

"... you're supposed to be here. God hears your complaints about time, which is why you need to hear God's secret, so you can expand your time, live the great life God has 'in store' for you, and, so you can enjoy each moment of your life and each person in your life. God wants you to have it all, all of the time, for the rest of your time, your life. To learn how to have it all, do you have time?"

"Yes, but..." he hesitates. *"How can you tell me what my concerns are when we just met a couple of minutes ago?"* He's being so funny, so human, I have to laugh: *"That's easy. During the past two minutes you have already confirmed you have no time to have a life, let alone a moment of time to be with God, so you can hear God's plans for your life and begin to live the great life God intends for you to live. You have also shown me what it is like for anyone to try and gain a moment of your time."*

The man is smiling, as the President of the National Association begins my introduction, as the man inserts, *"I'm too busy to spend time thinking about my time. I know I don't have time to spend here today, unless you promise me what you are going to say will help me with my daily life."* I'm almost out of time, but I do what I can to assure him: *"God's secret about time will give you back your life. In fact, you don't have any more time in your life to miss out on what God has 'in store' for you."*

He stands with a puzzled look, as he mouths the words *"... (motioning to himself) don't have any more time in my life to miss..."* while he is motionless a moment.

"You are not alone," I continue, *"many people are so busy being busy, they are always talking about being out of time, while their life actually passes them by. I understand, because my life used to resemble your life. Our conversation is one more confirmation that we all need God's secret to expand our time each day. There is a lot more for us to do while we are here on this earth. So, do you think you can spare a few minutes of your day, today, less than one hour, to hear the secret, so you can expand time in your life?"*

"What? Nobody can expand time." The disbelief in his voice is apparent. With a smile, I respond, *"No human can, but with God we can expand time. We just need to know God's secret. If you will spend a few moments of your time with me right now, I will share God's secret with you. Does that sound like a fair deal? The choice is yours."* Security staff motion the 30-second signal, as the man walks backwards, smiles, and says *"I'll be listening to every word and if I do find out how to expand time, I will let you know after your seminar."*

"See you in a few minutes..." was all I needed to say before I walk across the stage as the music volume increases and the people stand up and applaud.

We already have all of the time that we need 'in the world.'

Shocking, and yet, it's true.

God has already provided all of the time 'in the world' that we could possibly need. It's a done deal ... really!

It is the desire of God's heart for us to live aligned with ***God's Storehouse Principle*** so we will begin to hear and see what God has 'in store' for each of us.

We start by tithing our time. Six minutes from every hour. A minimum of 2.4 hours per day.

Continually, we talk about time. We complain about time.

Our conversations are filled with our thoughts about how little time we have while we repeatedly spend time talking about the lack of time in our lives!

I had not noticed the high 'loss of time' percentages before God showed me. I started watching time lost during calls from people explaining why they have not had enough time to complete a project. Sometimes they stayed on the phone for nearly an hour.

Sad but true, I've often heard friends state a long list of reasons why they had no time to share a statement with me 'at that time.' Many minutes later, the reason for the conversation is still missing and more time is being requested for them to discuss the purpose of the call. God help us with our problem! What is our problem? We are steeped in being human, accepting / repeating the lies!

Psalm 34:10 (NIV)

The lions may grow weak and hungry, but those who seek the LORD lack no good thing.

But, Lord, we are so human! We spend a lot of time talking about lack, and we especially spend time stating that we lack time! In fact, we spend so much time talking about each situation where we ran out of time, we often run out of time to do what we are actually on this planet to do! We are such unique, funny creatures we must make God laugh!

Imagine, Jesus takes our hand to bring us home to heaven, while God shows us the purpose and plan for our life. How sad it would be for us if in that very moment, for the very first time we realize that we did not even begin to understand why we were on the planet, so we did not fulfill upon our purpose and plan at any time during our lifetime! And yet, our time is up! How would that feel?

The good news is: God has a BIGGER and better plan!

Jeremiah 29:11 (NIV)

For I know the plans I have for you," declares the LORD, "plans to prosper you and not to harm you, plans to give you hope and a future."

God provides what we need, and He will never forsake us!

Living aligned with ***God's Storehouse Principle*** is how we will be able to turn **all** of our situations around. So, we have to find the time to begin the process! To live an 'extra' ordinary life, we need to 'expand' our time so we can find the 'extra' moments required to live an 'extra' ordinary life. To do this, we need to know and begin by living our life per God's truth: God gives us a new day each day, a 24/7 life!

Time With God Changes Everything

Before the journey, my prayer requests were laundry lists, merely words about my wants. In fact, I actually told God what I wanted God to do. Sad, but I was focused upon my needs above all else, and then, I told God exactly what and how I expected God to proceed, to 'get it all done for me.' Then, each day I re-evaluated how good God was doing during my prayers, based upon what He had accomplished on my prayer list! I was so human! I was focused on asking God to 'do it all for me.' I never saw my prayers from God's perspective. As soon as I did (the three visions God shared with me, within one night), everything I had prayed up to that point sounded lame.

Not an easy realization to comprehend, but, I had to remove all of the human training about praying and spending time with God. God had to show me that 'as humans' we do not know His word or that His promises are true so we are not able to comprehend the glorious things God has 'in store' for us.

1 Corinthians 2:9 (NIV)

... "No eye has seen, no ear has heard, no mind has conceived what God has ('in store') prepared for those who love him"

We have a very limited, human view of our life. I pray that status changes for God has a God sized view of our life. His plans for us are big.

So, how do we turn current time conversations around?

1 We start by tithing our time in a 24/7 schedule!

2 We stop living based upon the 8-10/12 hr. world based calendars!

3 We stop listing excuses for not "living" our 24/7 life!

Time has represented the same structure through the generations, remaining exactly the same through the centuries both prior to Christ and as of the Year of our Lord. God is absolutely 'in the details' about time!

The only 'break' in time represents the exact time Jesus Christ was on earth. In fact, all time is broken down into two segments:

All time BC: Before Christ
    Years prior to birth of Christ

All time AD: Anno Domini, meaning In The
    Year of our Lord (birth of Christ)
    Also Known As (aka) the line of time
    or, time line in the world

Everything we do while we are on earth, living our life, requires some of our time. Everything we want to accomplish in our life of time, aka lifetime, requires some of our time. Every step of the process, well, it requires our time.

So, who are we Aligned with?

How we spend our time, with whom we spend our time, and what we say about our life of time, our lifetime, is our choice. It is so easy to be tempted by the counterfeit!

Ephesians 2:10

For we are God's workmanship, created in Christ Jesus, to do good works, which God prepared in advance for us to do.

Matthew 6:33 (NIV)

But seek first his kingdom and his righteousness, and all these things will be given to you as well.

This lesson was learned slowly, so slowly due to repeating the problem it was often like walking over hot coals when God pointed out to me that I was not 'getting the point.'*

* A dear prayer partner, a former client and now Pastor, Greg Young, father of Collynn, identified a few times within ***It's A Faith Walk!*** invited me to be in his home while I helped with his business. At the time, his oldest daughter (Michelle) was about eight or nine. She had a strong prophetic voice at her age which was inspiring. She loved staying up late to hear the amazing things God was doing. Sometimes the details took a bit longer to explain to her than she had time to listen due to her bedtime curfew so she merely put her hands on her hips, looked at me eye to eye and asked, *"And, your point is?"* Sometimes we just have to stop all action, figure out the bottom line of the message and make the point!

Bottom line: To expand time we need to stop losing time by complaining about lacking anything, especially time!

Chapter 7 God's Storehouse Principle: Store Time

Storehouse for Time

The storehouse represents a special place or destination for our 'tithe of all,' and within the 'tithe of all' is our 'tithe of time.'

If you are saying, ***"What?"*** and your reaction is causing shortness of breath or heart palpitations right now, take a moment to breathe in a new, deep breath and let out the old thoughts / stuff in a big exhale. Fell better now? Good!

Now, while contemplating where that breath just came from, it is clear our ability to take a breath, each breath, is because God grants us each, new breath as one more breath of life.

Remember, we were dust before God breathed life into us! God supplies it, generously, while we do not, typically, labor to take a breath. Trusting you could say you hardly even think about the process or the <u>time required</u> because you are filled with an abundance of breath. In fact, you could probably confirm, easily, in your life ... there are many people (no need to make this exercise deeply personal) filled to the point they are 'full of it' or 'overflowing' with breath!

In the same manner, also, God gave us an abundance of time each day. We have the same 24 hours Jesus had, and we do not have to strap on our sandals and walk for miles each and every day. We do not have to seek lodging when we arrive. We have houses, cars and offices, all filled with 'time saving' conveniences, and we can easily, quickly take a shower after we return home from each journey and check messages from everyone communicating with us.

However, we are human! Important to remember this, because Jesus impacted the entire world before he arranged for us to do even greater things than he did during his brief time on earth!

However, in spite of all of the time God provides (many of us have at least two or three times the number of years Jesus had on earth), we continually allow ourselves to be in conversations about our 'lack of time' to live the life God intended, almost every time we are in a conversation. Sad but true, the people that hear it the most are the very people we proclaim to hold most dear to us, the people we speak to most often. Since God blesses us when we come together, denying that time or opportunity is possible or feasible our comments actually result in our proclamation of lies aka our denial of God sharing His blessings with us from His storehouse!

Becoming Grateful For Every Breath We Take

This is a good time to think about how often we live on 'auto pilot,' while Christ is 'in charge' of every breath while we are awake and while we are asleep!

I had the humbling honor to experience the last breath of life a dear friend took. Breathing was shallow for a few hours. God prompted me to check at certain points through the night. Then, at 8:45 AM she did not receive a new breath. Anne Boe passed away a few days before her 50th Birthday. Anne was also a motivational, keynote conference speaker. We created memories each time we shared special moments in time together.

Breathing a fresh breath every few seconds had become automatic, so it was not a thought that life is 'in the balance' of the brief moment in time before the next breath arrives. One moment Anne was here, alive, and the breath was evident. The next moment she did not receive a breath and in that same moment she was gone.

Each Day is a Gift from God

Each day is packaged and personally handed to us by God when we wake up each morning. In the first moments each day it is an honor to give 'first fruits / tithe of time' to God:

James 4:8

Draw nigh to God, and he will draw nigh to you.

We are always at a point of making our choice:

A. We can become a fully engaged participant in God's plan, fulfilling upon the purpose for our life through daily or hourly participation / involvement,

B. We can live as a witness or observer to time or life 'passing us by' while we are still breathing.

Question: Living per God's truth or the world based lie?

Results in your life: Are you 'Missing it' vs. 'Living it!'

Trusting you are becoming fully aware of the fact God has a bigger and better plan for you, and I pray light bulbs are going off, often, because it will make a huge difference while you are 'in the world' that you are not living 'of the world.' I pray you are choosing to be fully engaged in a BIG life plan!

What does time have to do with our Christian commitment?

While waiting for a client to arrive, a handsome man walked over to the bench where I was sitting (in the natural, it was really the voice of the Holy Spirit speaking through him, helping me 'get it').

In the gentle voice He is asking, *"Enjoying your time?"* I responded, *"I'm just waiting for a client."*

"It looks like a waste of your precious time." I do a few of my typical preoccupied gestures as I answer, *"I'm sure my client will be here soon."*

"Too bad a half hour of your time is already wasted today. Does this happen very often?" I am deep in thought, because He could be right. It does seem to be a frequent occurrence. People do tend to arrive late instead of arriving early. *"It happens. Traffic, phone calls, things come up at the last minute and affect the schedule."*

"Yes, I know it happens for other people. How you have spent your time is what I am wondering about. Are you a Christian?" He asks. *"Yes I am,"* I say with a bit of pride in my voice, *"I attend church on a regular basis."* To myself, I wonder why I am defending the fact I'm a Christian by stating I do go to church as He explains, *"I am asking a personal question about your pledge to God. I am not asking you about your church attendance. We are having church right now ... whenever two or more are gathered together, Christ is in the midst."*

"Right. I agree." My words are spoken, but, He does not stop talking. *"Attending church is an opportunity to spend some time in God's house. Most Christians just sit in a church a few minutes each week. I am asking you about your personal time, because God has a purpose for each moment in time. God knows how much of life is spent being Christ like. Do you know how much of your time is spent living Christ like?"* He asks.

Wishing my client had arrived as I think about my time. *"I do spend a lot of time as a Christian,"* I reply nervously, before I fully take in the statement He just shared. With little hesitation I continue moving my mouth, before my brain shifts into gear, *"In fact, I work with the leadership of churches and ministries around the world. I go church to church as Paul did, encouraging pastors, and I do the same work with businesses. God sends me nation to nation."* He interrupts, *"Are you more like Paul or more like Christ when you encourage pastors?"*

"Probably more like Paul, since the work is the same work Paul did with the churches, encouraging the people, the leaders, the pastors, so they can remain steadfast in their faith and operate in the church as God provided the structure within the scriptures." Now He appears to be deep in thought, so I just keep talking, *"I try to be a good representative of Christ while I am working with them ..."* as He interrupts and asks, *"Are you only spending time trying to be like Christ when you are with people or are you living as a good representative of Christ in your daily life which other people observe?"*

A bit, OK, a significant bit of hesitation before I reply. It was only a silent moment or two but it seemed like a long, long time before I said, *"I pray I'm a good representative of Christ every day..."* He smiles and calmly says, *"God knows if you represented Christ in the past half hour. Do you think you did?"* My pause lengthens, *"Well ...* (gathering thoughts) *I hope I take the opportunity to represent Christ ... "* He begins to laugh as He says, *"Don't worry. God will give you time to figure it out. You are fortunate because God is forgiving. He loves you. He gives you extra time and second chances. It's sad but true, many Christians have become so busy with their personal life they are actually living their lives upside down instead of right side up."*

Making hand motions about upside down, as I ask, *"Upside down? I could be living my life upside down? I think I am doing everything God wants me to do. How can I be sure if I'm living my life right side up?"* He provides a drawing (giving me a vision to see the structure) to help me as He answers, *"Life is upside down when all of the world's details and daily issues are your # 1 focus, and when there is any time left in the day, it is quickly filled by needs of everyone in your life, your family and friends. God gets what is left over or nothing when you are exhausted and ready to crash at the end of the day.*

World News, Issues, Career, Worries

Relationship, Family, Friends

God

The structure makes sense. It can tip over at any moment. He continues, *".Your life is not balanced. You are ready to fall over at any moment and in any situation! When your focus is upon the world and everyone that asks for your time, it leaves you with very little time if any to spend with God."* I sat, stunned, as He continued: **"An upside-down life has no stability. A breeze can blow you over! It often resembles the feeling of our gears in our life being stuck in neutral, with the engine running and the gas** pedal on the floorboard, when nothing seems to be going right. Bottom line: The harder we try, the less we accomplish."

As Christians we need to remember the truth:

God 1st and all else shall gain proper perspective!

"A right-side-up life is stable, and remains stable, while we go forward in the plans God has in store for us, even if strong winds blow! God asks us to focus upon Him, first, our immediate family and friends, second, and our relationship with a job, colleagues, and the details about the world, third. Then, our life is balanced, and we are ready, willing, and able to stand firm at any moment, armed and ready to do battle!"

God

Relationship, Family, Friends

World News, Issues, Career, Worries

The vision is clear.

The structure is solid.

This plan represents a life built upon the rock.

When we spend all of our time thinking about the news, our worries and details in the moment it becomes much easier to be stern and respond in a judgmental way:

Matthew 7

Do Not Judge: "Judge not, that you be not judged. ² For with what judgment you judge, you will be judged; and with the measure you use, it will be measured back to you. ³ And why do you look at the speck in your brother's eye, but do not consider the plank in your own eye? ⁴ Or how can you say to your brother, 'Let me remove the speck from your eye'; and look, a plank *is* in your own eye? ⁵ Hypocrite! First remove the plank from your own eye, and then you will see clearly to remove the speck from your brother's eye. ⁶ "Do not give what is holy to the dogs; nor cast your pearls before swine, lest they trample them under their feet, and turn and tear you in pieces.

Keep Asking, Seeking, Knocking. "Ask, and it will be given to you; seek, and you will find; knock, and it will be opened to you. ⁸ For everyone who asks receives, and he who seeks finds, and to him who knocks it will be opened. ⁹ Or what man is there among you who, if his son asks for bread, will give him a stone? ¹⁰ Or if he asks for a fish, will he give him a serpent? ¹¹ If you then, being evil, know how to give good gifts to your children, how much more will your Father who is in heaven give good things to those who ask Him! ¹² Therefore, whatever you want men to do to you, do also to them, for this is the Law and the Prophets.

The Narrow Way: ¹³ "Enter by the narrow gate; for wide *is* the gate and broad *is* the way that leads to destruction, and there are many who go in by it. ¹⁴ Because[a] narrow *is* the gate and difficult *is* the way which leads to life, and there are few who find it.

You Will Know Them by Their Fruits: ¹⁵ "Beware of false prophets, who come to you in sheep's clothing, but inwardly they are ravenous wolves. ¹⁶ You will know them by their fruits. Do men gather grapes from thorn bushes or figs from thistles? ¹⁷ Even so, every good tree bears good fruit, but a bad tree bears bad fruit. ¹⁸ A good tree cannot bear bad fruit, nor *can* a bad tree bear good fruit. ¹⁹ Every tree that does not bear good fruit is cut down and thrown into the fire. ²⁰ Therefore by their fruits you will know them.

I Never Knew You: ²¹ "Not everyone who says to Me, 'Lord, Lord,' shall enter the kingdom of heaven, but he who does the will of My Father in heaven. [22] Many will say to Me in that day, 'Lord, Lord, have we not prophesied in Your name, cast out demons in Your name, and done many wonders in Your name?' [23] And then I will declare to them, 'I never knew you; depart from Me, you who practice lawlessness!'

Build on the Rock: [24] "Therefore whoever hears these sayings of Mine, and does them, I will liken him to a wise man who built his house on the rock: [25] and the rain descended, the floods came, and the winds blew and beat on that house; and it did not fall, for it was founded on the rock. [26] "But everyone who hears these sayings of Mine, and does not do them, will be like a foolish man who built his house on the sand: [27] and the rain descended, the floods came, and the winds blew and beat on that house; and it fell. And great was its fall." [28] And so it was, when Jesus had ended these sayings, that the people were astonished at His teaching, [29] for He taught them as one having authority, and not as the scribes.

Then, He says, *"Now that you know how to focus your time during your day and figure out whether or not your time and your schedule are in balance, how does your time schedule for today, especially the past half hour, look to you?"* I reply while thinking about how simple He made the diagrams and the message: *"Not very good."* I'm thinking about every minute lost within the half-hour that was wasted today. *"Don't worry about the past half hour, just do better in the next few hours today, and tomorrow, and each day, OK?"* He says anticipating my response. Deep in thought: *"I will absolutely do better by tomorrow."*

He asks, *"Do you want some help putting the time schedule into perspective?"*

"Yes, please, what is the best way to turn the schedule around?" Smiling, He says, *"It helps a lot to know when you are*

able to expand your time versus wasting your time. We waste time whenever we live our lives according to our own personal plans. We can only expand time when we are in relationship with God, blessing other people and meeting needs, as God directs."

Not realizing it, I boast with pride being quite evident, *"Well, at least I never tell God no."*

"Not so fast. It's human nature to tell God 'no' more often than we tell God 'yes'. In fact, few people say 'yes' to God. You were ignoring God just a few moments ago. How we spend each moment of our life confirms our commitment. We are either aligned with God or denying God. So, let me ask you again, are you sure you are saying yes to God? Seems like a trick question, so I'll give you a few examples of how people respond by saying 'no' to God:

Commitment	Denial
Yes Lord, is a Yes	No Lord, is a No
	No time right now.
	No time to think about it.
	No time to do anything.
	Not now, maybe later.
	Not now, I'm too busy.
	When I have more time, l will ____.
	Out of time today, maybe tomorrow.
	Too tired to think about it right now.
	If I could find the time, I would ____.

People with more time should ____.

Maybe later today I could ____.

Maybe tomorrow.

Maybe later ... maybe ..."

As the list gets longer and longer and longer within the vision the first words of denial disappear as the new items are added and I hear myself saying every single response to God 'over time' in my life, I sink a little further into the hard, old, wood bench. This is so embarrassing, I thought, while I was realizing that my perception of always saying, **"Yes,"** to God and thinking I am always willing to do what God wants me to do ... it was actually me **stating the lie** about my time **to me, and to God.**

So I asked Him, *"How can I turn this around? I do not want to deny God. I want more of God. I want to spend my time the way God wants me to spend my time. How can I do this?"* He started with, *"...what God has given to you each morning is a brand new, 24-hour day. No world-based calendars include every hour from midnight to midnight."* Wow, the first time I worked out a 24 / 7 calendar, it required four pages of columns for the days of the week, and on the left side I only listed the hours in 15 minute segments on each page:

1) midnight to 6 AM,

2) 6 AM to noon,

3) noon to 6 PM, and

4) 6 PM to midnight.

The World / Enemy Lie Is Evident In The Calendar

The schedule that has been unfair to us is actually the 'world-based' eight, ten or 12-hour calendar. We try to squeeze everything into one-third to one-half of each day of our life. Then, the weekend days are only represented as half days or they are do not exist, Saturday or Sunday.

To God, the calendar is unacceptable. The calendar is a lie! To put the calendar into perspective we need to see the 24 hour day for all 7 days. The format is provided briefly, above, and it is expanded into the full day schedule with 15 minute segments within each hour in the workbook.

When each day is broken down into 15 minute segments, it requires four pages to represent the 24 hours of each new day.

Once we shift our focus, peace returns and we can insert the highlights of our life within the hour, so I have also provided the hourly, 24 hour calendar in hourly segments within the workbook for each week.

Hopefully, 24 hour / 7 day calendars will be in 'high demand' in the near future.

It would be great to have all of our friends and co-workers living a full, 24/7 life with us!

Bottom line: Until we spend time more time with God, we are not going to know God's plan for our time or how we are to contribute our time or plan our blessings which we are going to contribute to others!

I Corinthians 2:9

"Eye has not seen, nor ear heard, nor have entered into the heart of man the things which God has ('in store') prepared for those who love Him." **(NIV)** *"...for ear hath not heard, nor eye seen, nor can the mind begin to conceive the glory God has 'in store' for those who love Him."*

God has seeded our lives and the lives of fellow believers with all that we need to fulfill upon God's plans for these days.

When we put the entire 24 hour day in front of us and we mark the day starting with the most important time we schedule, our time with God and we specifically identify time with our family and the significant people in our lives, we will begin to realize that we still have plenty of time for our career. Soon, we will be enjoying the progress we are noticing vs the former status when our focus was on the worries we carried with us hour after hour, day after day, all of the details which burdened us each moment / hour of our day. We will finally be able to 'let go and let God.'

Exactly as the famous commercial states:

When you begin your day: Got God?

As you progress through your day: Got God?

As you end your day: Got God?

James 4:8

Draw nigh to God, and he will draw nigh to you.

The truth:

When you do draw close to God, you will have extra time.

A tithe of all: It's not just a money conversation!

To participate within ***God's Storehouse Principle***, aka God's contribution cycle, we need to know how we are to seed 'a tithe of all,' because 'a tithe of all' (that we have and we are) is a much bigger conversation since it is about far more than a 'give some money to a church on Saturday or Sunday' conversation.

We have been influenced by the world / the enemy and over time we have become affected due to compromising with the world regarding tithing and planning.

'A tithe of all' is absolutely a tithe of all that God has 'seeded' within each of us, and then, the added blessings God has given to us over time.

It's a process, and for us to know how to proceed, we have to find time to plan 'a tithe of all.'

This is why we needed to learn that we have to expand our time, and to do that we need to understand and live ***God's secret about time: Expand, Store and Tithe Time.***

To tithe properly, we need time to prepare our heart and mind to hear God's plan. We need more time to plan, to produce and to contribute our tithe of all including all that we are and all that we have become. Then, more time is required for us to be discipled and for us to disciple others to do the same process, while we also require time to live our life, aligned with ***God's Storehouse Principle.***

Seems like a lot of time. Yes. It is! It's required for God's preparation to fully equip and train us since God's plans for us are

BIG! To live BIG with God, we need to live according to God's secret about time.

A Moment in Time Becomes the Difference Between Life and Death!

A dear friend remained close with multiple calls and emails each day. Then, without notice, the emails and phone messages were going to her but I was not hearing back from her so I stopped.

God wanted me to call her. Without realizing it, I started telling God how I had remained in touch but she is not responding. God was insistent that I needed to call her.

Finally, I dialed her number. When the call went to voice mail, I became a bit prideful while I was actually telling God, *"See, I was right."* God remained insistent that I leave a message, in fact, a prayer.

I started praying. Then, God told me to tell her, *"**God is giving you a new song.**"* God was being so insistent, that I was saying it before I thought about it. I continued the prayer while God was telling me, again, to tell her, again, *"**God is giving you a new song.**"* I must have sounded a bit apologetic that I was repeating myself when I told her what God wanted me to do and in God's own way the words were coming out of me, again.

As I continued to pray, God told me to tell her *"**God is giving you a new song**"* a third time. And, I found myself explaining that God wanted me to call and give her this message three times.

Then, I did not hear from her for a few days but, when she called she was in tears. She was telling me about the prayer. She could not talk to me then. She was so sick, she could not lift her head or breathe deep enough to speak a word. She was laying near the phone. She heard me through the voice mail system and she was so grateful but she was too weak to even try and pick up the phone.

Moments before the call she had cried out to God to know if she was dying. Since she used to be a singer, she made a deal with God. She told Him if she was not dying He needed to send three confirmations that he was giving her a new song. She wanted to laugh when she realized how quickly God sent the three confirmations within the one prayer I prayed during the voice mail message but, she did not have the energy or breath to do anything beyond thank God from her heart and go into a deep rest with God while He healed her and continued to fill her with His breath of life. Honored to realize God's promptings confirmed life vs. death.

It happened another time when I was prompted to call a dear prayer partner in the exact moment which caused her to realize she was unable to form words let alone state a phrase which made any sense. She needed to arrange to go to the hospital. I was trying to do everything possible over the phone which would save her the costs of going to the hospital. I did not receive a separate message from God, as I was only prompted to call her at that exact time and during the call she became aware of what she would not have known if she was not trying to talk to me. Her inability to talk was due to experiencing a stroke in that very moment.

She did go to the hospital and she found out from the Doctor's that her blood pressure was so high she should have been dead. Ah, the comforting words of the Doctors. But, God ... in the moment of need ... directly provided her with the truth and then sustained her and continued to breathe life into her until she reached the hospital and heard the facts about her health condition. Per the Doctor's confirmation, she had already lived well beyond what human comprehension could understand based upon the facts of how quickly a stroke progresses.

God's plans for us are life, not death; truth, not lies; blessings flowing believer to believer keeping the body of Christ filled to overflowing with powerful testimonies to encourage each member to keep on keepin' on by faith.

Why is time the first tithe of a tithe of all? Because!

When you spend more time with God, God will spend more time with you and seek you out during your day a lot more often. Plus, God's surprises, words of knowledge and wisdom, are priceless. The result becomes an awesome life for us and a contribution cycle to enjoy living with all of the people!

Trusting you may want to spend some time with God right now. Take as much time as you want. I'll meet you at Chapter 8 when you are ready.

Chapter 8 God's Storehouse Principle: Tithe Time

If you look back over your lifetime, you will see how everything in life happens 'at the appointed time.' So, how do we figure out the mystery of time? What do we need to do with our time once we have it back? # 1 We need to tithe our time.

Tithe of Time

24 hours per day. Tithe = 2.4 hours per day

.1 hour, 60 minutes = 6 minutes

So, the .4 hour = 24 minutes

Tithe of time each day = 2 hours and 24 minutes

Time in prayer, reading the bible, listening to counsel of the Holy Spirit, as Christ directed, and, contributing to others:

Contribution of Time cycle = Storehouse Principle: Time

Contributing time to the people and plans we hold dear.

Do not panic!

In the beginning, until you have enough practice:

Daily tithe can be 'caught up' within the weekly tithe:

Time with God during the Sabbath.

Remember: Honor the Sabbath and Keep It Holy!

A day set aside at the end of the week, the 7th day.

No time at the marketplace for food our purchases.

Staying with God and family or fellow believers all day.

Living Aligned: to the truth vs. the 'world based' lie

Time with God, especially while we are open to counseling by the Holy Spirit helps us live a great 24/7 day each day.

As we are often told to begin a financial tithe by 'setting aside' a tithe of our first fruits, it is the same with our time.

We start by 'setting aside' a tithe of our daily time from the first hours. It may take a bit of time to adjust to spending time with God each morning. To change our perception about our life and begin to experience the blessings of the storehouse, we need to shift how we view the first hours of each brand new 24-hour day.

I'm not talking about 2.4 hours of time. In fact, you can begin with a smaller percent. I already know the value and you will, soon, so feel free to start out slow and then, as soon as you hear God's whispers, you will want to increase to 10% and more & more, and include your spouse or the significant person or people in your life!

Personal time, first, then, fellowship time.

The truth: God's time schedule, 'expanding time,' provides for 'more than enough' time with God and our inner circle. The Holy Spirit makes each decision easier while we begin to adjust, to correct our focus / God's vision regarding our life! Then, in time, we get our life back, aka 'we get a life!'

The lie from the enemy resides within the world-based plan, the world-based calendars of only eight or ten or twelve hours each day. The pages make us think, over time, that we have to 'fill the hours' to 'be productive' and yet, by doing this, we lack time to do all God would have us do so we can:

1) Be in fellowship with God and our immediate and extended family,

2) Complete all of the work entrusted into our hands, our assignments / task(s),

3) Bless people we fellowship with: family, work, church, etc., and throughout the community.

What a difference the truth makes!

What happened to us? We followed the wrong lead!

When executives complain to me about time during our coaching sessions, they have a great memory about the lists of 'accomplishments' on their world-based calendars. They have memorized it, while they planned it, scheduled it and executed it, and I trust you have, also. They can easily repeat nearly every 8-12 hours of their business days for the past week! But, the remaining hours of their days and what they did with their family daily or during their weekend, the important details about their personal life, their relationships and their dreams ... it's a blur, if the memories even exist!

Why? Over time, we have aligned with **the lie**, the current, limited time within the 'world based' calendars. When we confirm we 'lack time' to be a blessing even to those we hold most dear, we are actually participating in **the lie** with the enemy and 'robbing' (the enemy steals, kills and destroys) from God, from God's plan for our life and from our family, friends and our life! Instead, we are to be a blessing in our life to all who are fully involved our life, to live a life filled to overflowing so we have the time to freely give / contribute our time to others especially to care for the widows and orphans (all women without husbands & all children without fathers).

We have a lot to do! We have a choice to make.

They will follow your lead! Where will you lead them?

Bottom line: We are either contributing / aligning within God's plan or we are contributing / aligning with the plan of the world / enemy, and if it is not clear to us in this moment, we need to seek the counsel of the Holy Spirit. We can also ask a trusted prayer partner, because they can easily look at our life / schedule and see what we do not see and they can confirm which choice we are making (or, we have made).

OK, I realize these words may appear to cause shortness of breath and heart palpitations, again, but, truth is truth, and within our schedules, therein lives the truth or the lie. So, when this happens, stop for 'a moment in time.'

Then, breathe in a deep breath of life, thanking God for our very breath / life.

Then, spend a moment counting the many blessings and thanking God for all God has done up until this very moment in time, today.

Did you stop? Did you breathe, yet? Did you spend a moment with God, yet? When you do, after you take in a new breath of life nothing about your life will look the same!

It is impossible to change our habits and our conversations until we realize we have to make the choice to shift. We need to be aware of our words within our conversations and we need to be careful about our choices because when we do, we will begin to find the time to tithe our time. From our 24/7 life we have time time to make our plan regarding how we are going to seed 'a tithe of all' God has placed 'in us,' so we become a storehouse of God's treasures.

Did you stop breathing again? I thought so. I'll wait until you catch your breath. This process is too important to miss a beat / breath for the truth is, we are God's storehouse, God's treasure! We are here to bless the people in the world with God's truth and our tithe. We are to schedule time to plan our specific seed / tithe. Then, arrange the time required to share it as a tithe of all that we are and all we have from all of the time God has given to each and every one of us! So, it helps us to realize the fact we are God's participants in God's plans, as God's hands and feet involved directly with God every hour of our day to fulfill upon God's plan. **God provides enough time!**

Which moments do you remember?

How many moments 'in time' are epiphany moments?

How many epiphany moments from yesterday do you remember?

If the percentage is so low that it would not even register on the charts, then God's secret is going to continue to bless your socks off, as you share your 'tithe of all' with God, with you & yours, and with all in need as God so directs! A process which will help us look at our years on earth: Down the left side of a piece of paper write the number of each year of your life. Below each number write the words:

Birthday

Memories Created

People Who Created Memories

Insert the memories you have regarding your birthday and then memories you created for other people.

Then, add the names of people in your life who created memories for you.

At this point you may think you have to exchange the people in your life for new people. However, your perspective may change when you reach the end of each decade of your life, identify it and answer these two questions about the decade:

------------Decade of life

Who discipled you during this decade?

Who did you disciple within this decade?

 # 1. Invite God into your daily schedule

 # 2. Invite you back in, and the people you hold dear,

 # 3. Invite the other people (your Network, and then, the work and activities that truly help you fulfill upon your purpose and plan for your life!

Bottom line:

God provides enough time

when He receives our 'first fruits' of our time!

Chapter 9   God's Storehouse Principle: Cash Flow

God's Currency

God's plans are not based upon the currency of any nation. God confirmed this when He sent me to London seven times within a 12-month period. I left with a $5 bill in my wallet and I returned with the $5 bill in my wallet.

I thought it was strange.

God clearly confirmed it was His plan.

God was proving to me that I was traveling / living based upon His currency and not the currency of a nation in the world. Due to his orchestration of details and provision in many nations, I can confirm we need to learn how to live according to God's Currency, a much more efficient and prosperous process!

God was not referring to cash amounts calculated for barters, God was talking about providing a tithe of all that He has seeded in us and provided to us so all shall be blessed.

Due to the current status of the global economy, I wish the body of Christ was already operating based upon **God's Currency,** aka *God's Storehouse Principle.*

Compromising with the World Causes Problems

<u>**A basic currency lie**</u>**:** Credit being built per the world plan <u>**in truth**</u> equals increased debt! We were not to become debtors. The world created the 'credit score plan' so we would think we are building high levels of credit, but this is **the lie** because we are becoming deeply indebted.

If you are wondering, *"How can I pay the debt?"*

I'm not meaning to sound cliché about this, but the quickest answer: *Schedule more personal time with God!*

I appreciate the quote by Frederick Franson, not because he and his Swedish family lived in Nebraska when they came to America, but because of his commitment and effort in establishing the Evangelical Alliance (his history is available on the internet). He passed away in 1908, so I trust you know I did not meet him personally but his quote remains with us to encourage us: *If you are sick, fast and pray; If the language is hard to learn, fast and pray; If the people will not hear you, fast and pray; If you have nothing to eat, fast and pray.* (Many examples in *It's A Faith Walk!*)

The plans God has for you are to prosper you!

Deuteronomy 5:33 (NIV)

Walk in all the way that the LORD your God has commanded you, so that you may live and prosper and prolong your days in the land that you will possess.

1 Kings 2:3 (NIV)

... and observe what the LORD your God requires: Walk in his ways, and keep his decrees and commands, his laws and requirements, as written in the Law of Moses, so that you may prosper in all you do and wherever you go,

Psalm 1:3

And he shall be like a tree planted by the rivers of water, that brings forth his fruit in his season; his leaf also shall not wither; and whatsoever he does shall prosper.

Romans 13:7-9 (NIV)

Give everyone what you owe him: If you owe taxes, pay taxes; if revenue, then revenue; if respect, then respect; if honor, then honor.

2 Kings 4:7 (NIV)

She went and told the man of God, and he said, "Go, sell the oil and pay your debts. You and your sons can live on what is left."

Viewing all sources of income, as cash entering our life for our purpose and plan to be fulfilled!

The world has 'confused' us about credit and debt. Since we are told to 'build up a high level of credit' but, credit cards or credit lines or equity lines because having increased credit limits are made to sound very good however, everything about higher credit levels truthfully equals increased debt!

So, by saying to us we are gaining credit even though extended credit hurts their 'credit score level' and if we spend more than 50% of the credit amount the 'credit score' decreases, so the truth is the world process of exchanging the word debt with the word credit makes us debtors and therefore the credit plan in the world is **a lie.**

God wants us to live debt free and to cancel debts.

Deuteronomy 15

"At the end of *every* seven years you shall grant a release *of debts*. [2] And this *is* the form of the release: Every creditor who has lent *anything* to his neighbor shall release *it;* he shall not require *it* of his neighbor or his brother, because it is called the Lord's release. [3] Of a foreigner you may require *it;* but you shall give up your claim to what is owed by your brother, [4] except when there may be no poor among you; for the Lord will greatly bless you in the land which the Lord your God is giving you to possess *as* an inheritance — [5] only if you carefully obey the voice of the Lord your God, to observe with care all these commandments which I command you today. [6] For the Lord your God will bless you just as He promised you; you shall lend to many nations, but you shall not borrow; you shall reign over many nations, but they shall not reign over you.

From All Income Sources

Whether it is a monthly paycheck or two, or cash coming in (income) from multiple sources, we are to shift our thinking to consider all income appearing as Cash Flow, a.k.a. 'Flowing Cash' into and through our daily life to fulfill upon God's purpose and plan for today (and, God's plan is to prosper us, also).

Watch for Temptations from Every Angle!

The world tries to tempt from every angle.

In the world, life can appear to become tight and frustrating.

So, companies offer a 'deal too good to be true' for only a few dollars a month. The deal is 'too good to be true' as is.

They work diligently in advertising and marketing campaigns to convince us to spend the cash since it is merely a few dollars per month.

There is no mention of the pay off amount.

There is no focus upon the fees and interest added.

The temptation becomes too much because the deal looks so good, so if we are not careful the bill is added to the monthly budget because it appears to be 'available' cash.

Your Income is to be Treasured
It is your Treasure to Disburse, to Bless You & Others!

It requires a different format to help us gain a new way to think about CASH IN than to think of immediately where the cash needs to go before it arrives, for a bill to be paid, a.k.a. CASH OUT.

CASH IN (from one or multiple sources)

10% Tithing account

10% Savings account

____ Entertainment account

____ Weekend "get away" account

____ Vacation account

____ Contribution account

____ Tax payment account (property/state/federal)

____ Retirement plan account

____ Health benefit (deductible) account

____ Insurance (auto/home, deductible) account

CASH OUT (include all costs for each item, within one line item amount)

____% Home (Mortgage, Ins., Maint., Taxes, Utilities, Improvements, etc.)

____% Auto (Payment, Ins., Maint., DMV & Lic. Fees, Fuel, Wash, etc.)

____% Health Care (Insurance, Preventative, Gym, Nutritional, etc.)

____% Education (Courses, Books, Training Programs, Seminars, etc.)

____% Debt (credit cards, personal loans, additional debt, etc.)

(add your categories)

Family Plan

Credit: Mom and Dad grew up during the depression. When credit cards became available they would only use them for specific needs, i.e., travel or a store purchase, and only if they were able to pay off the balance at the end of the month. They would not do anything to become 'indebted.'

Tithe: If Dad had to work in the field when we left for church, he talked with Mom about the tithe amount. The payment was prepared and they prayed over it together, before he went to the field and Mom took us to church.

What Are We Accomplishing By Doing This?

Changing the focus from 'paying the monthly bills, per month, each month' with nothing 'extra' to show for all of the effort, to establishing a 'PAY OFF PLAN.'

Interest Only = Increased Debt and No Equity

The world has convinced millions of people to accept 'interest only' plans. This plan does not pay off anything and it results in no equity. The cash you pay merely results in interest being paid to the lender.

The temptation point is easy to identify. Paying only the interest amount makes the payments appear to be lower so the lender convinces you to accept a higher purchase amount than you would accept if you were paying off the principle.

Pay Off Plan

Cash Flow toward the Pay Off Plan requires converting from focusing upon the world / budgeting bills), to our hope and future by planning the income flowing to pay off / cancel debt; shifting the bottom line focus from the amount of the monthly bills to the amount of the entire 'pay off' of debt.

The world has affected millions of families by having them use all of their 'equity' in their homes which started the loan over for another long term pay off plan and all fees were added, again. Many of the families obtained the equity line to improve / remodel their home and then they lost their home when the value changed. Are you seeing a few of **the lies** the world promoted which caused families to be affected?

You have probably observed similar problems which the world has created for you or someone in your family. Planning each day to achieve the goal of assets being free and clear with -0- debt and -0- indebtedness.

Again, since hindsight give us 20/20 vision regarding our finances, assets and debts, we need to back into the Monthly, Weekly, Daily Flow of Cash. We view the Cash Flow as it CYCLES IN & OUT of our life. We begin by planning the adjustments required to shift from indebtedness to -0- debt or indebtedness.

Take good care of your cash.

When I was traveling with God without an extra coin or tunic, I was often asked to submit a check for my donation / tithe to a ministry 'as a record' but God has been very clear with me, *"I am not a tax deduction."*

This was a new concept for me, as the churches and ministries have always kept a close record and provided a year end statement or summary of the donations so people can use them for tax filing purposes.

We need to be responsible and keep our own records for the tithe / plan / taking action will be clear because we are fully engaged now vs. following man's plan ... a process that is separate from God's plans.

This being said, it is clearly defined in the Bible that we are to pay unto Caesar what is due Caesar.

What Would You Do With A Million Dollars?

You do not have to wait to find out. God focuses upon the entire amount. We need to do the same. Surprising, but earnings before deductions quickly add up to a million.

The time to figure out what you will do with your million is now!

MILLION DOLLAR GAME

In our lifetime, we actually handle a million dollars, or two or more.

At $20,000 per year, it would take 50 years to earn our million, and at $50,000 per year, it would only take 20 years, without one increase in pay/1

A plan should be in place to confirm how we will benefit the most from our million(s). This is why the million dollar game is established, once we know how to proceed with a cash flow vs. a budget the bills plan. Focusing upon our personal $1,000,000 plan changes our perspective for each purchase decision and each dollar we spend.

Overall plan for our cash flow to represent something in life vs. copies of bills paid is confirmed within the MILLION DOLLAR GAME.

The game supports focusing upon how to pay off our home, vacation home, auto(s), and all of the indebtedness in life, to LIVE a BALANCED "Extra" ordinary LIFE!

Chapter 10   God's Storehouse Principle: Planning

Failing to plan is actually planning to fail.

1 requirement for planning:

Schedule time to plan!

2 requirement to plan:

Establish a plan!

3 requirement for the plan:

Proceed upon a God inspired, life plan!

2 Corinthians 9:8 (NIV)

And God is able to make all grace abound to you, so that in all things, at all times, having all that you need, you will abound in every good work.

Proverbs 16:3 (NIV)

Commit to the LORD whatever you do, and your plans will succeed.

Proverbs 16:9 (NIV)

In his heart a man plans his course, but the LORD determines his steps.

Proverbs 19:21 (NIV)

Many are the plans in a man's heart, but it is the LORD's purpose that prevails.

Psalm 33:11 (NIV)

But the plans of the LORD stand firm forever, the purposes of his heart through all generations.

GOALS FOR TODAY:

'To Do' list of each of the DAILY DETAILS

Random lists of activities and tasks are OK, since it is more important to include each activity and task as you think of it, so you are sure that each one is on the list!

Planning process is the next step, while it is important to remember: more and more tasks and activities will be added, as each hour of the day unfolds and the week progresses.

You can begin with a blank piece of paper while the form in the workbook includes options to remain 'flexible' while making the list. This is done to support your personal "flexible" cooperation!

RESULT: Quickly prioritize the variety of activities and tasks to be completed today, and/or another day in the week/month, when an item is not a top priority for today. Within the workbook, the form helps accomplishing the tasks and activities during the day, the week, and/or the month.

Blank paper or on the form, the page(s) are not rewritten as each item is completed. It is 'checked off of the list' when 'it is finished' since each of the many activities and tasks added during the day / week / month shift the original priorities.

PROCESS: Topics on the list. Scroll down the list and select the most important items and write # 1 in front of no more than five items. Prioritizing the items with # 2 on the next five, # 3 on the next five and so on will help keep the plans in perspective, until you have prioritized each of the items.

When you add items and/or pages, as the hours of the day and days of the week progress, you will need to take a few moments to review the items, and to prioritize them and/or re-prioritize the remaining items on your list.

This process becomes easier each time to begin a new list. When you complete each item, put a heavy line through it and a check mark on the right. On the form, I title that column 'it is finished.'

When each item is checked off of the list, and the appointments are complete, the page can be filed with your daily, weekly and month plans, until the end of the month.

Regarding: Cash Flow plans. The weekend getaways, etc., need to appear within the details of your plan! Items requiring attention for the monthly event, a special weekend or an event during the week, need to be included and prioritized with your tasks and activities.

GOALS FOR THIS WEEK:

Summarize the key tasks and activities from the "to do" list, the goals for each day, and include the events planned or special plans made for each day of the week.

"Insert" the working time, the key points of the day and the week, the goals and accomplishments planned for the week, and the personal time, the planning time, and, of course, the hours proceeding upon the goals and activities, and the hours of rest!

ADD:

Weekly financial goals based upon the 5th, the 10th, the 15th, the 20th, the 25th.

NOTE the TOP Financial Plans for: Personal / Family / Business Goals, Monthly Events, Trips, Vacation, etc., with:

Weekly Schedule of Contributions to _____

Contributions to Personal / Business Plans _____

Contributions to remaining bills, etc. _____

Actual Dollars Available _____

Dollars 'set aside' for current or future Event(s) _____

NOTE the TOP Plans, People & Resources:

TOP - Plans for Personal LIFE

TOP - 'Planning' items in daily/weekly/monthly LIFE

TOP – Action ('In Action') items in daily/weekly/monthly LIFE

TOP - People in daily / weekly / monthly LIFE

TOP - Resources in daily / weekly / monthly LIFE

TOP - Plans for Business LIFE

TOP - 'Planning' items in daily/weekly/monthly LIFE

TOP – Action ('In Action') items in daily/weekly/monthly LIFE

TOP - People in daily / weekly / monthly LIFE

TOP - Resources in daily / weekly / monthly LIFE

GOALS FOR THIS MONTH:

'To Do' Summary of LIFE PLAN key points for the Month.

OVERVIEW of the Monthly Plan, including TOP daily, weekly and monthly plans, events, people to meet with and share time and projects with, and the key points of the month, including the top activities and tasks for the Month.

Monthly PLAN, summarizing the Daily Goals & Weekly Plans:

TOP Financial Plans for:

TOP - 'Planning' items in monthly LIFE

TOP – Action ('In Action') items in monthly LIFE

TOP - People in monthly LIFE

TOP - Resources in monthly LIFE

Chapter 11   God's Storehouse Principle:

Talents, Skills and Abilities

Life is filled with talents, skills, abilities and resources.

1 - Recognizing our ability, and the ability of the other people in our family and our life, and in our business and industry to make a contribution.

2 - Making a contribution, individually, together with family, with other people in our life, including professional colleagues, within our business and industry.

List of Talents, Skills and Abilities:

Natural Talents: Trained Talents:
1.   1.
2.   2.

Natural Abilities: Trained Abilities:
1.   1.
2.   2.

Natural Skills: Trained Skills:
1.   1.
2.   2.

List of Training:

    Schools

    Courses

    Seminars

    Certificates

Summary of TIME devoted to contributing natural talents, skills and abilities:

Daily

Weekly

Monthly

Summary of MONEY invested in training to improve talents, skills and abilities:

Daily

Weekly

Monthly

People who would benefit from these Talents, Skills and Abilities:
1.
2.
3.
4.
5.
6.
7.

8.

9.

10.

11.

12.

These people become the twelve people to begin discipling!

Congratulations!

Chapter 12   God's Storehouse Principle

People, Networking, Resources

Proceeding step by step, *'Networking Through Six Degrees of Separation.'*

PEOPLE   *'Six Degrees of Separation'*

List three to seven people in your life and in communication with you (think of each level as one circle in your life, expanding out to include the levels of relationships within your life, so you include all of the people impacting your life):

PEOPLE – 'involved' in your LIFE, each day, every day, inner circle:

1.
2.
3.
4.
5.
6.
7.

PEOPLE – 'involved' in you LIFE during your business day, next circle:

1.
2.
3.
4.
5.
6.
7.

PEOPLE – 'involved' in your LIFE, during the week, next circle:

1.
2.
3.
4.
5.

6.

7.

PEOPLE – 'involved' in your life, during the weekends, next circle:

1.

2.

3.

4.

5.

6.

7.

PEOPLE – 'involved' in you life, on a monthly basis, next circle:

1.

2.

3.

4.

5.

6.

7.

PEOPLE – 'involved; in your life, on an occasional basis, during the year, next circle:

1.

2.

3.

4.

5.

6.

7.

PEOPLE – 'involved' in your life, on an infrequent basis, during the year, next circle:

1.

2.

3.

4.

5.

6.

7.

PEOPLE – the 'additional' people 'involved' in your life, the people who are 'hearing life details' make up the next circle:

1.

2.

3.

4.

5.

6.

7.

Now, the truth becomes evident in the process.

1. Put a check mark next to each person knowledgeable of your dreams, goals and LIFE plans.

2. Put a circle next to each person you need to inform about your dreams, goals and LIFE plans:

3. Put an X next to each person supporting your dreams, goals and LIFE plans 100%:

4. Put an * next to each person questioning each decision you make:

LIST:

1) All people with a check mark and an X, and add each of their names on separate days of your monthly calendar, with the intention to call, email or communicate with each person.

2) All people with a circle and an X; be sure to inform them of your dreams, goals and LIFE plans.

3) All people with a circle need to hear about your specific dreams, goals and LIFE plans, so they can support or question you about your dreams, goals and LIFE plans.

4) All people with a circle and an *; identify the plans they are not aware of, and then decide if the person should know more about your plans or less about your life and any of your plans.

5) All people with an * need to be identified and a decision needs to be made regarding identifying and discussing the negative impact they may have upon your personal and/or business life, and how often you want to be in communication with them prior to discipling them and / or if God confirms you need to dust off your shoes and discontinue regular contact with them.

REPEAT the above for LIFE & Business Resources: vendors, clients, staff, employees, peers, supervisors, commuters, etc., etc., etc., to be sure all people are included.

PHASE 1:

Identifying the people that influence our life from each 'level / circle' of life, the people 'at the core' of daily life, from the inner circle to the people seven levels out from the inner circle. These people and the people they are networked with make up your six degrees of separation that connects you to everyone. **People involved in daily life, from most frequently involved to less frequently involved, identified within each of the seven levels of circles.**

PHASE 2:

Identifying the top three or four people in each level, and the <u>three</u> to <u>four</u> topic(s) of conversations from two categories:

1) Tasks, concerns, problems, or issues you are facing in your life,
2) Plans or goal(s) that are important to you and to your life plan.

Listing the people and topics, as the patterns of each level and type of influence are identified.

NOTE: Additional topics can be identified, while it is best to not list more than seven at this time. Goal: top three!

The top three or four topics in each category should be addressed first.

Then, the next three or four topics can be addressed in the same format.

PHASE 3:

Beginning with the # 1 topic of tasks, concerns, problems or issues:

'Y' for YES by each # 1 next to the name of each person, if the topic has been discussed.

'N' for NO by each # 1 next to the name of each person, if you have not discussed the topic.

'?' by each # 1 next to the name of each person, if you think the person is aware of the topic, however, you are not sure if you have discussed the topic.

Continuing the process until the list is complete for # 1, then for # 2, and # 3, and # 4 topic.

Then, begin with the # 1 topic of plans/goals, and repeat the same process, and then, with # 2, # 3, and # 4.

Part 1: Circle all 'N' topics, and transfer the information onto the 'N' page, noting only the people with 'N' marks identified, and then proceed to the next phase.

Part 2: Circle all '?' topics, and transfer the information onto the '?' page, noting only the people with the '?' marks identified, and proceed to the next phase.

PHASE 4:

After the people on the 'N or the '?' lists are identified, select the people to schedule some time with, to discuss the topic or plans identified.

Add the names and phone numbers to the 'To Do' list and prioritize the time on the 24 hour calendar based upon the same process as the items are scheduled within the TIME section of the workbook.

Keep the lists for each phase, from identifying the names to listing the topics and plans to discuss with each person.

PERSONAL RESOURCES:

Family and friends in the same industry:

People in the same industry:

Family and friends in the same position:

People in the same position:

People in the same company, in the same position:

Business or professional associations for the position:

Professional resource people for the position:

Training seminars, centers, colleges, etc., for the position:

BUSINESS RESOURCES:

Businesses in the same industry, in the community:

Businesses in the same industry, in the country:

Businesses in the same industry, in the world:

Business or professional organizations established for the industry:

Training seminars, centers, colleges, etc., established for the industry:

TIME & MONEY planned and/or invested in PERSONAL RESOURCES:

TIME & MONEY planned and/or invested in BUSINESS RESOURCES:

NOTE: Sometimes it may seem like we need to <u>replace everyone in our life</u>, while it is critical to remember our lessons in life are typically for our benefit and the opportunity to learn may be based upon discipling the 'problem' people.

Chapter 13   God's Storehouse Principle: The Game

Balanced Life Game

PERSONAL LIFE GAME

ONLY Three TOP items to focus on during this day:

Personal LIFE items/plans to focus on

1., 2., and 3.

Intimate Relationship LIFE items/plans to focus on

1., 2., and 3.

Family & Friend items/plans to focus on

1., 2., and 3.

Daily LIFE plan items/plans to focus on

1., 2., and 3.

BUSINESS LIFE GAME

ONLY Three TOP items to focus on during this day:

Management LIFE items / plans to focus on:

Time/Money/Resources

Financial LIFE items/plans to focus on

Marketing items/plans to focus on

Daily Business LIFE items/plans to focus on

PERSONAL & BUSINESS LIFE GAME

ONLY Three TOP items to focus on during this day:

Personal LIFE & Management LIFE

items/plans to focus on:

Intimate Relationship & Financial LIFE

items/plans to focus on:

Family & Friends & Marketing

items/plans to focus on:

Daily LIFE & Business LIFE

items/plans to focus on:

EACH GAME BOARD:

Decide:

Between each of the categories.

Are you "IN" or "OUT" of balance?

Rank: (is your life currently a 1 or closer to a 10)

Personal, from 1-10

Business, from 1-10, and

Combined Personal / Business LIFE, from a 1 to 10.

Game boards for each are on one page. After the process works well for the Personal and Business boards (usually takes a week or two to grasp the concept and see the flow) the combined board is all you need to prepare in the morning.

Easy to complete the boards, confirming your plan for the day within three to five minutes each morning, are provided within the workbook.

God's Storehouse Principle walks us through the daily process to quickly produce a clear, concise, workable plan for your daily life! The result is a plan that is easy to change and adjust as your plans change, minute to minute, during the day. Bottom line: Get into the game and live an "extra" ordinary balanced life!

Results in: Balanced Life Game which begins when we shift our perspective on time, to a 24/7 personal daily focus vs. the world based 8-12 hour calendar day, with half days or no days represented for Saturday or Sunday. A 24 hour/7 day calendar, includes the time required for planning time, which can easily be identified within a full 24/7 life schedule represented each day of the week.

Each chapter, Time, Cash Flow, Pay Off Play and Million Dollar Game, Planning and Resourcing our Talents, Skills, Abilities and Resources, Networking Through Six Degrees of Separation, and Planning, resulting in 'Living the 24/7 Balanced Life Game: Personal, Business and Combined,' while the training shared walks you through the process and provides the tools, techniques, and forms required, since they do not exist in the marketplace, today. The support is provided to help you shift from the current, limited forms and ordinary life, to enjoying 'extra' moments, cash, resources, networking resources and planning options within each of the areas of our life, to live an 'extra' ordinary life.

This is the first step in 'jumping into the game of life.' Here's to you, and to your personal success becoming evident to you and to everyone in your life as you begin to participate in *The Balanced Life Game* which is based upon **God's Storehouse Principle.**

The book and workbook are designed to become an easy way to comprehend and then give the discipleship gift to each friend and family member, so they will have the same opportunity to comprehend the process and easily complete *The Balanced Life Game* board within three to five minutes each day. God's plan is powerful and I trust you will also be living a balanced 'extra' ordinary life, soon, very soon!

I have faith in your abilities! God does, too!

Question: When you prepared your calendar for this week, did you insert your time with God 1st? If not, quickly go back – remember, God loves us and gives us 2nd chances!

I pray you are seeing the truth: your testimony opens the eyes and ears of all who are lost, when you share the facts, the truth about how God blesses you and your life more often, which will continue to re-encourage you to bless more people and spend more time with God and the people that mean the world to you.

It's a contribution cycle, God provides to us for our life and stands with us, while we learn to let go and our life expresses LIFE to / for / with others! Within a short period of time, I trust this will be your conversation when you meet other people and share your testimony with them. Then, the truth will be your testimony as it becomes one of the testimonies of all of the people being blessed by you and by each of the people your life / testimony touches each day.

Did you make your personal time & time with those you hold dear your next priority? If not, quickly go back – remembering (with a smile?), God gives 2nd chances!

OK, is the schedule starting to look like you have a blessed life? Great! (I already know how the 'new plan' feels!)

The good news:

God gives us a new day, every day, and an entire lifetime to LIVE and complete the plan!

Each morning, just for fun, pretend God is looking over your shoulder as you seek time to spend with him and then the time to devote to your life and the life moments which are precious when they are spent with those hold most dear!

The truth: Soon you will forget you are pretending because God is really with you, looking over your shoulder!!!

Congratulations!

Now, live it and pass it on and expand your inner circle so **all** around about you will also experience HIS Best!

Sheila

Chapter 14 God's Storehouse Principle: Discipleship

Keep On Discipling!

Discipleship and New Assignments

God's Daily Plan:

Discipleship

Accept new assignments

1.

2.

3.

4.

5.

6.

7.

8.

9.

10.

God's Storehouse Principle:

Keep On Seeding / Harvesting!

Reality Check

Realignment with God's Storehouse Principle

Planning/Preparing

1.

2.

3.

Seeding/Nurturing

Harvesting/Storing

Replenishing/Planning

1.

2.

3.

(cycle begins, again)

My Commitment

My commitment to you in this moment is the same commitment I make to each person attending the seminars and conferences around the world, and to all of the people in churches where I'm invited to preach: I'm here for you, standing firm with you, in truth, for we shall become 'more than conquerors' **Romans 8:37** Power and authority multiplies when we align with God, and come together to fulfill upon His purpose and plan for these days!

Personal request: Find one person each day to share God's secret with! Enjoy seeking out seven new people per week. One per day. That's all I ask.

My Prayer for Us

Each time you read these words they will have a deeper impact upon your life, your family / lineage and your sphere of influence in your family, circle of friends and colleagues in your church, business, industry and community, while it blesses you as much each time you read the words as it did the very first time for God's truth holds gems which we discover the deeper we enter into relationship with Him.

Isaiah 40:31 (NIV)

...but those who hope in the LORD will renew their strength. They will soar on wings like eagles; they will run and not grow weary, they will walk and not be faint.

May it be well with your soul in this hour, in these days, while you find 'extra' time to be with God, to bless your life, and to bless all in need of your time, skills, talents, abilities, resources and all God has provided to you & seeded in you!

May your heart and mind open up to God's 360 degree viewpoint vs. our 'human limited' 90 to 180 degrees 'off course' thinking!

May you realize options for blessing others and find that our 'more than enough' God has granted 'more than enough' time for us to share the blessings: time, income, planning options, people, resources, skills, talents and abilities. May we always find ways to share who we are with others, as God directs us to disciple and to be discipled for all of our days of our LIFE. And, may someone come forward to help us insert discipled and discipling to be accepted in spell check options automatically as demonized and demonizing are so easily accepted, already! *Lord help us remain close!*

Faith Walk and Discipleship

The walk of faith is not always easy, especially alone and without discipleship but, when we spend focused time with God each day and we share / contribute our time to disciple and encourage each other our time, and our life, expands. In **III John**, the expression of love Christian to Christian is expressed clearly within the letter sent to Pastor Gaius (in the Amplified version):

3 John 1:2

Dear friend, I pray that you may enjoy good health and that all may go well with you, even as your soul is getting along well.

May we find time for our expressions to be similar when we speak to one another confirming 'Peace be with you' as we depart for the Peace passes all understanding! God has confirmed when I have nothing else to say, tell the person *"Bless you"* for then the Holy Spirit will remain with them and do a work beyond what I could do 'in that moment' for them.

Truly, I am honored to be one of God's servants available within this hour, to bring you this message regarding how our daily habits are related to the results in our life, so we will produce a mighty harvest in the world, and in our life, so our human experiences while doing kingdom business aligned with Go's will, will truly 'become on earth as it is in heaven.'

Our Commitment

Together, we are the true servants of God, the true representatives as an ambassador for Christ. We can stand firm and fight against the wiles of the devil, alone, since we wear the whole armor of God (Ephesians 6), remaining aligned with God's will, and we are even more powerful when we gather as two or more believers to fellowship together with our Christ in the midst.

Our Prayer

"Lord, You hear our voices and You know our hearts. As humble and able servants we are willing to tithe time and all that

we are and have to You each day, and to other people and to their needs as you direct, to accept the promise Christ provided to listen to and follow the counsel of the Holy Spirit. Father, thank You for keeping Your hand upon us and aligning our will with Yours, for the gift of a new day, every day, for more time to be with You, to plan our day, our life, our future, and to bless others. Thank You for our life and for the gift of hearing Your voice clearly as we walk in faith while we are still here on earth. In the mighty and matchless name of our Lord & Savior Jesus Christ we pray, Amen

Become Ready to Take On An Assignment

When God extended me in London past the date of the frequent flier flight ticket date I was granted a unique itinerary with a return flight to California routed through Chicago instead of New York. I tried and tried to make the airline staff change the ticket, but all they would say is *"it is done"* so I was going to be changing planes in Chicago.

Due to the extensive global travel, I have become familiar with the New York airport and the terminals involved in the changing planes process. Chicago was a new adventure and upon arrival the adventure looked a lot more like a life-altering challenge.

When I finally got to the gate (OK, it's also important to note that I had been on flights for nearly 24 hours by the time I got to Chicago and anything that resembled how I looked when I departed on the original flight was not even a memory I could bring to mind when I saw myself in the mirror upon arrival in

Chicago), I was waiting in the line to confirm my boarding pass when God prompted me to turn around.

I told God I do not know anybody in Chicago so there is no reason for me to turn around. However, God became a bit more persistent with each prompting to the point of shocking me and I reacted by turning my head quick enough for the people behind me to see the condition of my face and hairstyle. In the exact same second while I was shocked I had turned my head and I was trying to find my sunglasses to diminish my 'look', I heard a man with a deep Spanish accent saying: *"Septiembre, Septiembre, Septiembre!"*

Every ounce of my being did not want to look up, but God was prompting me to look up and acknowledge the man. As I tilted my head up slightly and glanced at the people in line behind me, I realized Pedro Ibarra, his wife and interpreter were directly behind me in the line. They were with Carlos Annacondia in San Diego a few months before. As I trust you have guessed, it was during the previous September.

The Holy Spirit had to be confirming who I am to him, also, since the 'look' of me after nearly 24 hours on flights clearly did not resemble the woman they met during the meetings the previous September!

They were on flights for the same length of time. They were very tired and completely dehydrated. God has orchestrated 'water packing' for my many journeys, so I had enough water left to share with with them. Their appreciation confirmed they were blessed beyond measure. God was busy. The interpreter spent the entire time trying to get both of us to slow down so he could have time to translate!

If you ever get a chance to hear Carlos Annacondia speak, go early and stay late! The Holy Spirit fire (fuego in Spanish) is hot! As he walks across the platform saying, *"Fuego, fuego, fuego ..."* deliverance happens without making a personal request; many set free within moments. Blessed to be a witness. Many times when he was invited to be in San Diego, California he brought Pedro Ibarra, the officer over all of the Assembly of God churches in South America. What a pair they are when they preach! If you ever get to hear them as a 'tag team' you will be mightily blessed.

Empty Vessel so God can Fill Us!

God wants to fill us as an empty vessel. It's just not that easy for me to become 'empty' very often! I thank God that He accepts me as a 'work in progress.'

May it be an easier process for you!

The assignments often happen due to God prompting me to call someone. I've shared two examples which resulted in life vs death for two dear prayer partners. Since you may be the only person who makes the call when God makes the request, I pray you will devote the time to HEAR His voice and accept His assignment(s)!

John 10:7-10. Jesus the Good Shepherd

Then Jesus said to them again, "Most assuredly, I say to you, I am the door of the sheep. [8] All who *ever* came before Me are thieves and robbers, but the sheep did not hear them. [9] I am the door. If anyone enters by Me, he will be saved, and will go in and out and find pasture. [10] The thief does not come except to steal, and to kill, and to destroy. I have come that they may have life, and that they may have *it* more abundantly.

Honor God's Commandments

A key commandment is: We are to honor the Sabbath and keep it holy. Whether we choose Saturday or Sunday, instead of arguing and isolating from any of the fellow believers, even though sundown Friday to sundown Saturday is a blessing that will change your life and the lives of all of the people you know, does the day you choose seem like a holy day?

Currently, we are placing so many demands upon the businesses on the day of Sabbath while we are to prepare 'in advance' so we can spend the holy day of each week as a day separate and set apart.

Instead of eating out, prepare food for the family or some food to share with fellow believers so the fellowship time is not causing people to keep a cafe open or work to serve us on that day.

Some Christians are not able to get the day off or even part of the day off to worship with fellow believers which is frowned upon by some within the denominations. However, the problem is that too many of the Christians are the very people causing the businesses to be open and involve their staff on that day. We can change this as of this weekend!

I pray you are beginning to see what is possible because as the body of Christ we can stand together, assist each other and change this status in a heartbeat, also known as (aka), as of this weekend!

Live per God's Word in Fellowship

Build or re-structure the church upon the apostles and prophets with Christ as the Chief Cornerstone.

Ephesians 2:19-21

Now, therefore, you are no longer strangers and foreigners, but fellow citizens with the saints and <u>members of the household of God,</u> [20] <u>having been built on the foundation of the apostles and prophets, Jesus Christ Himself being the chief cornerstone,</u> [21] <u>in whom the whole building, being fitted together, grows into a holy temple in the Lord,</u> [22] <u>in whom you also are being built together for a dwelling place of God in the Spirit.</u>

Live per God's Word as Fellow Believers

We are to feed the lambs, especially the widows and orphans. Whether the widows have a pension or not or whether they end up on the street, homeless, and whether the children are in an orphanage or in the foster care system or dealing with the strained situations within a single mother (or grandparent) household. The question is: *What are we accomplishing on their behalf?*

Does it seem like as a fellowship of believers we are doing God's will?

If you want to see a great example of what one woman can do in one town with the children of the street, a great example is Heidi Baker!

Have you heard about the ministry of Heidi Baker? God is doing amazing things through Heidi for the current and future generations. Her ministry is **Iris Global** and her website is that name .org. There are several powerful videos on You Tube. She's been on TBN and there are several videos on the internet available through God Tube, also.

Remember how stuck you used to feel before realizing the plans you made were completely upside-down?

Trusting you can see what is wrong now, and you are beginning to see ways you can participate in turning it all around, right?

It Is Not Enough To Only Know Right From Wrong

Briefly and basically, we compromised with the world and while we kept compromising we lost track of what was right per God's word and what was wrong. In fact, I heard a great definition which is better than knowing right from wrong. Since the devil is the closest counterfeit, this definition is much closer to the truth:

We need to know the difference between what is right and what is not quite right.

How Do We Learn to Live per God's Storehouse Principle?
We have to be willing to live per

>**God's commandments: Honoring all 10, especially**
>>Honor the Sabbath and Keep it Holy
>
>**God's word:** Follow God's commandments.
>>Feed the lambs with the truth and bread of life.
>>
>>Care for the widows and the orphans.
>>
>>Aligned with God's will; guided by Holy Spirit.

Personal note: In the midst of the unique and sometimes 'appearing to be a bit traumatic' details of the past two decades, a man impersonated a real attorney who happened to have the same spelling of his name.

Before he crossed my path, he had destroyed many lives and families and escaped after stealing funds and destroying their lives easier and than Houdini due to the fact he was not the real attorney so he never had to face the people he destroyed after his fraud scheme devastated their lives.

What he did within seven days of meeting me was so horrific, a dear friend, a witness and Registered Nurse (RN) said, *"I hope he dies the most horrific death."* I asked what that was like. She said the person begins convulsing; they are unable to clear up anything in their life because they cannot speak; their convulsions cannot be controlled.

Result: The man passed away exactly 30 days after he met me and immediately began his plan to impact (destroy) my life. He spent his last seven days in the hospital experiencing the most horrific death experience.

The RN told the details to an attorney friend.

He called to tell me a miracle happened. When I called to hear about the miracle, he said, *"God added an 11th commandment today!"* You can imagine my excitement as I asked him, *"How did it happen? What is it?"* He said, *"God's 11th Commandment is: 'Thou shalt not mess with Sheila Holm' ..."*

Hebrews 4:12

For the word of God [is] quick, and powerful, and sharper than any two edged sword, piercing even to the dividing asunder of soul and spirit, and of the joints and marrow, and [is] a discerner of the thoughts and intents of the heart.

We have to be willing to put on the full armor of God.

Ephesians 6:10-20. The Whole Armor of God

Finally, my brethren, be strong in the Lord and in the power of His might. ¹¹ Put on the whole armor of God that you may be able to stand against the wiles of the devil. ¹² For we do not wrestle against flesh and blood, but against principalities, against powers, against the rulers of the darkness of this age, against spiritual *hosts* of wickedness in the heavenly *places*. ¹³ Therefore take up the whole armor of God, that you may be able to withstand in the evil day, **and having done all, to stand.** ¹⁴ Stand therefore, having girded your waist with truth, having put on the breastplate of righteousness, [15] and having <u>shod your feet with the preparation of the gospel of peace;</u> [16] above all, <u>taking the shield of faith with which you will be able to quench all the fiery darts of the wicked one.</u> [17] And t<u>ake the helmet of salvation,</u> and <u>the sword of the Spirit, which is the word of God;</u> [18] **praying always with all prayer and supplication in the Spirit, being watchful to this end with all perseverance and supplication for all the saints** [19] and for me, that utterance may be given to me, <u>that I may open my mouth boldly to make known the mystery of the gospel,</u> [20] <u>for which I am an ambassador</u> ...

As I mentioned in ***It's A Faith Walk!*** God had a lot of 'on the job training' to do after he equipped and trained me as I was kind to people, I did nice deeds and I prayed God would not forget my name. But, I was clearly not learning how to 'get it done' within the first few decades of my life in church Sunday after Sunday (the number of decades is not relevant, so the exact number shall remain anonymous).

The Holy Spirit Provides the Truth in the Moment
Voodoo Princess
Attempts to Curse Me Off the Planet

During the first night of a Spiritual Warfare Conference at Earl's Court in London, a unique woman sat next to me. She continually disrupted the service.

Of course, she chose to do this while I was trying to enjoy the songs my friend and pastor Earl Harrigan was singing. I kept praying, but, she continued to be disruptive to the entire front (ministry) rows of the meeting.

God confirmed, *"She does not belong in the meeting."* I told the security staff. They noticed she was wearing a badge, so they said she does belong in the meeting.

After the service, the woman was marching the perimeter of the building, inside and outside. I mentioned the details to the security staff, and I confirmed again that God said she does not belong in the meeting. They said, *"If she returns tomorrow night, just point her out to us and we will talk with her."*

The next night, the very minute she arrived she asked me if she could sit next to me again. I told her it had been very disruptive the night before and I really wanted to hear my friend sing tonight. Then, I pointed her out to the security staff since they said that was all I had to do and they would talk with her.

But, they told me I would have to walk her to the Director of Security. So, I did. I kept praying as we walked. The Security Director wanted me to show him what she was doing the night before. I told him I'm not going to act out what she does. It was clear he did not want to deal with the situation so I told him what God told me, *"God said she does not belong in the meeting."*

He asked me for proof. So, as I continued to pray, I said what God instructed, *"Ask registration."*

When he checked, he found out the woman was not registered for the meeting.

Registration handed her a badge and she wrote her name on the badge due to the fact she was disrupting the entire entry area of the meeting the first night so instead of the registration staff speaking with her, they merely let her enter.

Security did not want to take action, so I prayed with greater fervor (or fervour since I was in London), "**God help me!**"

God prompted me to face the woman directly and hold my arms up to protect the hearts of the (12) security guards. God directed me as I spoke directly to the woman, "**Since our Lord is confirming you do not belong in this meeting, I'm asking you if Jesus is your Savior?**" She smiled, as she coyly and pleasantly said, "**Yes, Jesus.**"

The Director of Security is busy confirming she was quoting scripture to him and now she is confirming Jesus.

I kept praying, as I needed direction from God about this. God confirmed, again, she does not belong in this meeting. So, I asked God for the words, and God showed up powerfully!

Through me, God said, "**Who is the closest counterfeit? Does he reside in you?**"

She lunged toward me and her face became contorted, as though she was pressed hard against a large partition (Jesus and the angels) between us but, she was not able to speak and she did not have a voice … she was muted.

Frozen, nothing was moving, not my lips or my mind! Then, I heard God say, open your mouth, so I did and I was immediately speaking with intensity, "**I'm a favored representative of my Lord and Savior Jesus Christ and anything you want to say unto Him, you can say to me now.**"

Again, she lunged toward me but she was stopped hard and fast by Christ as the invisible barrier between us.

Her face became contorted again, and she was unable to speak.

So I asked her, *"If you choose to be in the meeting, you can choose Jesus Christ as your Savior and remain in this place. But, if you do not choose Jesus Christ as your Savior, you must depart from this place. If you choose Christ you will be assisted and supported by everyone here. So, the question is: Do you want to choose Christ now to be free in your life and remain in the meeting?"*

She reared back, rose up high, and spat at me. Her spit was stopped by the invisible partition between us.

As the guards were the witnesses we could each see it dripping down but it was not able to get to me.

Then, I said, *"If you do not choose Christ as your Savior to stay in the meeting then you must leave but, these men will be gracious with you and escort you to the door. My prayer is that you will choose Christ and stay but, you have to declare your choice in your own voice as the choice is yours."*

She reared back and in a full, deep and loud guttural voice as many have shared Satan sounds she said, *"He who curses me shall be further cursed!"*

At that very moment, the Security Director said, *"OK then, she has made her choice."*

Immediately, he directed security staff to quickly escort her out of the building. Then, they received reports that she started marching the perimeter of the building, so they walked her to the train station and they remained with her until her train arrived.

The security guards wanted prayers after she had left the building.

They wanted me to remove any curse, anything she may have spoken over them and I was honored to serve, to pray with them and provide the truth: A Christian church is built upon the prophets and apostles with Christ as the chief cornerstone!

The men were completely unaware of the fact that the woman, even though she attends a church in London, and she says the name Jesus, and she actually quotes scripture, she is not a follower of Christ. Instead, she is attending a Satanic based church.

Most of the men knew the location of her church since it was located very close to their churches. They did not know the congregation which took over the church building was not Christian. Prior to this night, they were grateful a church was established in the building since the prior congregation was not able to cover their monthly lease.

By the way, if you have not realized they are over congregations and leading the people, I should mention this fact: The entire group of Security Guards involved (12) and the Security Director were pastors and senior pastors of local churches.

God introduced me around London in one short moment in time. And, God brought the truth to light about what we are dealing with in the world, "...*we do not wrestle against flesh and blood, but against principalities, against powers, against the rulers of the darkness of this age, against spiritual hosts of wickedness in the heavenly places."*

<u>Critical to put on the full armor of God!</u>

Epilogue

Getting a License to Live, Really Live!

Have you ever seen the movie **Secondhand Lions?** It is available at Walmart or Amazon for about five dollars and it is well worth the cost!

The life the two 'Secondhand Lions' lived was beyond comprehension per their relatives and neighbors, while they had no idea what the two men (Robert Duvall and Michael Caine) did to become so wealthy.

Their journey was an adventure of epic proportions.

Within the first few moments of the film, a great-nephew is dropped off to live with them and hopefully, for his mom's sake, find out where the two great-uncles have hidden their millions.

During the film, admiration for each of them grows and grows. They impact the future generation by providing the 'what every boy needs to know to become a man' speech.

They make such a deep and lasting impact upon their great-nephew that his final comment / testimony regarding the lives of his great-uncles: *"They lived. They really lived."*

I pray all who know you will be saying this about you, soon very soon, also!

We have a lot to do to shift our thinking!

In America, a pinnacle moment in life is when we pass the test and obtain a driver's license. In that moment it feels like independence and freedom are right around the corner.

However, the training phase is just beginning!

Remember what it was like to learn how to drive a car?

The driving instruction for 'safe driving' stated the requirement to align the middle of the front of the hood (sometimes there is an ornament) to the line on the right side of the lane / road. This one rule held our attention and focus while it kept the car in the right place within the lane.

Now, it's hard to remember which part of the road became the focus due to the fact the driving process becomes 'second nature' to us over time and we forget what it required to 'learn' so we could 'get a license'.

With practice regarding the exact instructions, over time, the ability to drive without watching where the center of the hood is pointing becomes our new reality. As we know now, I hope, if we are not following the right instructions even if they are close to being right the results are not the same.

We have to follow God's exact instructions as we flow within our life and within the body of Christ. If we do practice the right way, over time, while following the exact guidance of the Holy Spirit we can be formed by God into the specific vessel God intends for us to become during our lifetime on earth. Then, we can easily disciple others so our entire sphere of influence is 'in the flow of life!'

As Jesus taught us to pray for God's (not man's) kingdom to come and God's will to be done so it shall become on earth as it is in heaven, I trust you realize it was always God's desire for us to 'get a life license' so we know how to proceed in our life and we know how to live an 'extra' ordinary life.

The process of comprehending **God's Storehouse Principle** is exactly the same.

With God's guidance by the Holy Spirit, we will always be able to:

1. Expand / store / tithe and understand God's truth, His secret about time,

2. Expand cash flow and enjoy the pay off options vs. budgeting bills,

3. Expand the plan to have time to plan a tithe of all,

4. Expand our skills, talents and abilities to bless more people,

5. Expand the foundation / base of our life: people, network, resources,

6. Expand our daily LIFE plan with a 'Balanced Life Game', *

7. Expand our LIFE with continued discipleship and new assignments,

* God provides the structure to view all of life within a simple game board format. The plan for each day can be completed within moments each morning.

Bottom line: It becomes second nature for us to plan and implement a tithe from all that we are and have while we are living a LIFE aligned with and blessed by *God's Storehouse Principle.*

Careful: Leaven Alert!

Jesus confirmed with the disciples to not add to their words, as leaven (yeast, to make it rise) is added to bread. Communion, body of Christ, is unleavened bread.

Matthew 16:6

Then Jesus said to them, *"Take heed and beware of the **leaven** of the Pharisees and the Sadducees."*

Matthew 16:11

How is it you do not understand that I did not speak to you concerning bread?—but to beware of the leaven of the Pharisees and Sadducees ..."

Mark 8:13

[*Beware of the Leaven of the Pharisees and Herod*] And He left them, and getting into the boat again, departed to the other side.

Mark 8:15

Then He charged them, saying, *"Take heed, beware of the leaven of the Pharisees and the leaven of Herod."*

God's words and God's assignments are only what God ordains and orchestrates and **not one more ounce is to be added**, also known as (aka) 'no leaven' as Jesus warned the disciples to watch their words and make sure they only deliver the word and they do not add to the word.

A personal note 'just between us'

While we were in Ghana we learned an African worship song, a very special & simple message. It was shared by the praise & worship team from Bishop Duncan William's church:

ONE MORE TIME

ONE MORE TIME

HE HAS ALLOWED US TO COME TOGETHER

ONE MORE TIME

By the time we sang the verse for the third time, there was not a dry eye in the house!

I look forward to hearing from you, and hearing your details about the *'Faith Walk'* you are experiencing, or you have experienced!

Until we meet, speak and / or email the next ONE MORE TIME, enjoy the journey(s) shared in this book and the journey(s) God is and will continue to take you on! Then, write to me and share the testimonies of the glorious work our Lord is doing in your life.

Until the next ONE MORE TIME our Lord brings us together, as always, HIS Best!

Sheila

Email: hisbest4usorders@gmail.com

Web site: http://hisbest4us.org

Use the Subject Line: **God's Storehouse Principle**

Ephesians 2:19-22 *We are no longer foreigners and aliens, but fellow citizens... members of God's household, built on the foundation of the apostles and prophets, with Christ Jesus himself as the chief cornerstone. In Him the whole building is joined together and rises to become a holy temple in the Lord. And in Him you too are being built together to become a dwelling in which God lives by His Spirit.*

II Corinthians 12:14-15. (a) *"Now, I am ready to visit you...what I want is not your possessions but you...So I will very gladly spend for you everything I have and expend myself as well."*

II Corinthians 13:11-14. *Aim for perfection ... be of one mind, live in peace, and the God of love and peace will be with you. May the grace of the Lord Jesus Christ, and the love of God, and the fellowship of the Holy Spirit be with you all.*

ACKNOWLEDGMENTS

AFRICA

Ghana, West Africa

Pastor Sam,

"Truly, God has sent you to us with a strong word for our church."

Pastor Charles,

"It blesses my soul to hear of your faith & see the fruit of the ministry."

Johannesburg, South Africa

Pastor Jhanni,

"God is doing a good work through you and I pray with you & our church."

Coronation Ceremony

AMERICA

Dr. Jan Franklin, Georgia

"Thank you God for answering my prayers by sending Your apostle to (the region) to unite the believers ... "

Prophetess Nancy Haney, Alaska

"God has never given me this before. I see circles and circles and circles ... you drink and you draw from one circle to the other, and that's what you do, you drink and draw and you bring these circles together ... Pulling many groups together. All these groups need each other ... He can use you for you have ears to hear and you hear His

deep truth. You are filtering what is nonsense and what is real ... because you have been in that circle, and because of what you say they are going to merge. It is going to expand, become bigger than you could imagine."

Man of God (Georgia), Requesting to be Discipled while attending the coronation of a King in Africa, Georgia

"...at my age, it is hard to believe I am learning so much in these few days about what I did not know...realizing what it is to know that I know how it is to live within God's word each day. Will you consider discipling me?"

Pastor, Host of "Praise the Lord", TBN, **"...The fruit of the ministry is evident in your testimony..."**

International Prophet, **"You have remained steadfast to God's plan and God will continue to send you forth for His plan and purpose to be fulfilled, and for the thousands who have not knelt..."**

President, Christian Publishing Company

"Only God could orchestrate such a grand plan..."

Prayer Director, International Prayer Center

"God is opening many doors for you…"

Christian Publisher,

"God has given you a powerful voice and a sweet spirit…"

Pastor, Southern California

"God is raising you up and sending you forth to many nations…"

International Apostle

"God is doing a mighty work through you, for His righteousness precedes you, showers over you and follows you as a mighty wake. May it continue for each of your days…"

Prophetic Prayer Partner, Minnesota

"Only God could walk you through these days… accomplish so much through you, in the midst of your daily situations, the many blessings shared during each of your travels will continue to shower blessings upon each of the many households around the world…"

AUSTRALIA

Newcastle, New South Wales, Australia

Pastor Mark, "**...the staff and business leaders heard the message of Personal &Professional Life Management this week, so we are blessed you agreed to preach the word to our church this morning.**"

Prayer Team "**We know now how we will we be able to continue this mighty work when you are not in our midst...**"

Four Square Gospel Church, Aboriginal Cultural Center

Pastor Rex, **"God blessed us through your preaching on Easter Sunday. We will never forget that you were in our midst … God brought new people to Jesus today & we thank God for what He has done because you answered His call."**

ENGLAND

London, England

Pastor Vincent, Glory House, East London,

"…the honor is ours this Easter Sunday."

Associate Pastor,

"The Glory of our God Almighty shines upon you and through you in your speaking and your actions…we give Him praise."

Protocol Team,

"God has mightily blessed us, by sending you into our midst."

Pastor Arnold,

"You have blessed the people, and in His wisdom and timing timing, may He bring you back into our midst again, very soon."

Pastor, West London,

"We rejoice with you in hearing and seeing the mighty things God is doing."

Pastor, South London, **"Our God is evidenced in your life and your speaking, while we continue to thank God for the work He is doing through you..."**

High Commissioner, Kingdom of Tonga, serving in the Embassy in London, England; Ambassador, Akosita, **"God's timing is always right...for you to be with** us, prior to the Economic Summit, to meet and pray with us…"

Sunderland, England

Anglican, Former Church of Pastor Smith Wigglesworth

Pastor Day, "I thank God for sending you to our church this morning, for serving communion to me, and for renewing and restoring me for the call upon my life."

Kingdom of TONGA

Pastor Isileli Taukolo, "**Our board and business leaders were fasting and praying and God confirmed He was sending someone to us. We are deeply touched by the message God sent to us, through you.**"

Minister of Finance, Tasi, "**Our meeting was an answer to my prayers, and I thank you for providing the seminar for our senior staff members, and meeting with them individually for prayer and coaching.**"

Government Office, **"Thank you for speaking today and for staying and praying with us."**

Interpreter, Sela

Testimonials

Business to Business, Nation to Nation

B. Crousure, President
Medical Corporation

"Hiring Ms. Holm to help me structure my first business was the brightest decision I have made. She taught me how to understand what success demands of me and she trained me how to operate at her level of commitment, while expressing an intense passion for my life and for the business, and to significantly contribute to the community. Without her coaching, I know my wife, my team and I would still be standing squarely in the lackluster mire she found us in, today, instead of our business being rated on the New York Stock Exchange (NYSE). Her coaching techniques were the turning point for our lives and for our company. We have catapulted into and experienced fantastic growth, both internally and externally. We anticipated receiving help with business systems, however, her extensive experience in balancing every area of our life first, and then inserting our business into our life has made a huge difference in our life and our bottom line. Her depth of knowledge in life and corporate structuring has been the key to our success. As a lifetime athlete, I should have made the connection to what coaching would mean to my business. It has been the "play book", the two-hour training sessions, the chalk talks before the game, and the champagne after the victories!"

P. Long, Post Office Employee
United States Post Office

"Coaching is nothing like consulting! We have met with a few consultants about each of our business tasks and how the work flow should progress. However, when I attended our conference and heard about a speaker who identified specific coaching techniques which could positively impact each aspect of my life...I laughed and said, 'I will not be in that session'. Then, when I walked down the hallway, I realized something was going on, since the only place left in the room, was an opening to lean against the wall. I'm so glad I walked in...every aspect of my life has been impacted positively, since I heard Ms. Holm speak that evening. I thank you, and my family and my co-workers thank you!"

R. Oliver, Executive Vice President
Utility Company

"My staff had always attended the seminars, while I budgeted and selected the people to attend. However, I did not attend. I did not realize, until the first two hour session with Ms. Holm, I had always delegated the daily assignments at the office and at home, especially when I stated that I let my wife adopt two daughters. We

had help at home, I had help at the office, and all of the daily needs were met. However, I did not have a "extra" ordinary life! I did not have a meaningful relationship with anyone, including myself, until I met Ms. Holm. Nothing about my life is the same, since the first moments we met and I heard her speak about the TIME secret. I have gained an ability to relate personally to the people in my daily life. Our daughters now fight to sit closest to me. The results have been amazing, and I will always be grateful."

C. Lynch, Corporate Engineering Manger
Aerospace Industry, Entrepreneur and Owner

"I would still be working on my business plan and living without a life plan, for the first business instead of owning and operating three businesses today and enjoying an "extra" ordinary life, if I had not signed up for the Entrepreneurial Course with Ms. Holm. It was immediately evident in the course, I did not have a successful plan for my day, let alone a plan for my life, my family or my business. My business ideas were innovative, as I am a successful engineer and manager. However, I was not aware of the techniques required to establish a plan for my life or for my business start-up or the required steps to ensure the success of my business through the various development phases. The practical information and the step-by-step format of the coaching and the course made it possible to 'fill in the blanks' to establish my daily life plan, to fulfill upon my plans and goals, and to proceed with a

successful business plan and structure, while I was supported by the coach, and now, I can easily update my life and business plan each day! Many thanks, coach!"

T. Lehman, President
Furniture Manufacturing, Distribution and Sales

"The division we targeted for closure this month received our annual EXCELLENCE in Performance award for being our most improved division. Through your coaching process, causing each of us to create powerful life plans and then powerful plans for our work projects, teams automatically developed and began functioning effectively and <u>profitably</u>. The value of the staff believing in themselves far exceeds our initial intended results! The initial project resulted in a 50% increase in production and a 30% increase in related sales within the first 90 days."

R. Tretsven, Owner
Beauty Supply, with Salon Services

"Prior to hearing Sheila speak, I absolutely did not have a life! I progressed through each day, each week and month, fighting to keep ahead of the bills. Each time the business level plateaued, I went into a panic, a spin, and adjusted each section of the business, ie., I would stop ordering products, or reduce the number of technicians or sales staff, or obtain a new or expanded credit line. Everything about my business, and my life, were "out of control" and "out of balance." Then, when I tried the scheduling and budgeting techniques she described, I immediately noticed an increase of 35% in business, and 100% in life."

J. Schneider, Vice President
Interior Design Corporation

"We not only gained your level of passion and energy for our life, we gained the same level of energy and passion for our business and everyone who contributes to it. We are excited about the many techniques we learned, to search for everyone our business can contribute to within our community! We also profited significantly from the insights which surfaced, while we were creating our business, marketing and operational plans together. Thanks for believing in us during our periods of doubt, causing us to obtain the ability to create and proceed upon dynamic personal goals and then exceed all expectations by producing results beyond our previous three and five year plans within the first project plan. We have learned to 'not dig up with doubt, the seeds we planted in faith'. Thanks for everything!"

**T. Fakafanua, Minister of Finance
Kingdom of Tonga**

"Within the first 30 minutes of being introduced to Sheila, I scheduled a seminar and individual coaching sessions for our top 30 department heads and Treasury Department senior staff members. The timing was perfect, as we needed to restructure our policies, procedures and the entire operating plan, within the next 30 days. Ms. Holm provided a clear and practical outline for us to use, to structure our lives, our departments, and our government"

International: Business Adviser & Coach

Sheila Holm advises and coaches business owners and their management teams based upon God's Storehouse Principle. God does more in the lives of the people than provide immediate, positive, bottom-line strategies. The marketing and operations strategies identified specifically for each business and industry, produce profitable, long-term results. Sheila's clients track and report 30-230% increases, based upon their first working session. Her marketing focus on co-inventing the future of each business, evokes internal and external partnerships to immediately be identified and developed. With her dynamic leadership, each staff member and customer immediately recognize the changes in the business and they commit to expand their role in working in partnership with the business and the owner and team. Then, her ability to ignite dialogue and inquiry throughout the business, immediately causes leadership to emerge within the business and each partnership (i.e., with each staff member and customer) and expand into powerful business relationships.

Credentialed: Entrepreneurial Trainer, Seminar Leader, University Instructor & Educator

Ms. Holm was awarded an American federal contract to provide entrepreneurial training for executives within both the defense and aerospace industries where she trained engineers and top management from General Dynamics, Hughes, and Lockheed. The successful training program evolved into a copyrighted, credentialed, entrepreneurial training course. Ms. Holm established a panel of industry leaders to provide a management certificate program within the California University system and she is a recognized, international seminar leader. Recently, she conducted a seminar for 30 senior staff members within the Treasury Department of the Kingdom of Tonga and she became the advisor to the Minister of Finance and to The High Commissioner (Ambassador) of Tonga, in London, while preparing for the Global Economic Summit.

Keynote Conference Speaker, TV and Radio Celebrity, and Author

*Sheila has provided the keynote address for various professional associations and corporations. She is known for her "**Balanced***

Life Game" techniques (secular version of **God's Storehouse Principle**), and for her *"Networking Strategies"* topic, especially her *"Networking Through Six Degrees of Separation"* approach (included within **God's Storehouse Principle**), *which improves the success ratio for every conference attendee, especially first time attendees while meeting people within other businesses and industries within the working sessions and the conference EXPO. In addition, she is often asked to provide 'break-out' seminars throughout the scheduled conference days and the number of the attendee always exceeds the capacity of the room with people squeezing in, leaning against the wall and the water table in the back of the room.*

Her conference talks are known for being results oriented, action packed and exciting, while each person is impacted with a different insight, giving them the ability to develop a new awareness and understanding of their capabilities in life. She receives feedback from many of the participants that after attending one of her conference talks, they have finally realized how to practically reach their full potential. Because of her unique approach and her understanding of business strategies and industry trends, she has been interviewed on local, regional, national and international radio and TV programs.

About the Author, Sheila Holm

God's Storehouse Principle is based upon God's orchestration of all arrangements while God took Sheila's hand and traveled with her while equipping and training her and confirming ***It's A Faith Walk!*** The book by the title is a brief summary of about seven months of Sheila's three year journey after she surrendered and walked hand in hand with God, guided by the Holy Spirit each step of the way.

God has taken Sheila around the globe, going church to church, business to business, nation to nation. He directs her path to speak life into each situation whether God sends people to her to be re-encouraged or he asks her to pray with a pastor, the church, or someone in a store or a restaurant, etc. He fulfills upon His promises within His scriptures. He has equipped and trained her, while He:

- Sends her forth without an extra coin or tunic.

- Arranges flights and accommodations in each nation.

- Introduces her before she arrives.

- Lifts her up and encourages her.

- Seats her before governors and kings.

- Fills her as an empty vessel.

- Shares His wisdom and word of knowledge.

- Blesses and heals the people in her path.

- Comforts her and re-encourages her.

- Touches people individually in conferences/multitude.

- Speaks through her with power and authority.

- Addresses situations the body of Christ is facing.

- Speaks through her so the people hear His words in their own language.

Many confirm she walks in the five-fold ministry. She does not use a title because God does the work while He sends her as an apostle and prophet. God orchestrates all arrangements for her to preach, teach, and evangelizes.

Invitations to preach resulted in this book: **God's Storehouse Principle** with Foreword by Bishop George Dallas McKinney. The secular version of the book is **Balanced Life Game** with Foreword by Ken Blanchard.

When she preaches, God confirms that if churches will begin to shift from world based plans to God's plan by operating within **God's Storehouse Principle**, the church will be able to declare the church is blessed and then God's blessings will begin to flow to / through people, families & communities.

God has confirmed the scriptures again and again which confirm we are to be as wise as serpents yet gentle as doves. Sheila often admits the enemy has provided many opportunities for God's deeper training and her expanded growth. She was considered wealthy in the world before the rug was pulled out, but, she says she would not accept a dime for her prior life because God reached out his hand after she was forced on to a 2nd, 3rd, and 4th Social Security and Driver's license number while a case was being developed for federal prosecution of Superior Court Judges and trial attorneys.

Because she brought the truth forward about multiple injustices within the justice system, specifically the judges and attorneys committing fraud 'behind the scenes,' she was <u>promised</u> IF she changed her ID numbers her new record would be protected and she could proceed upon her one, clear and separate record. After two of the three judges and an attorney were sentenced to prison terms for Federal RICO charges, the agents did not concern themselves with the mess they created in Sheila's life: Their demands that she change her ID multiple times caused her to be unable to function in America. Agents ignored the facts.

The agents offered 5th numbers, but, she said, "Enough." She did not know the truth while they were insisting they were protecting her.

A clear and separate record was promised each time, but, the records were all merged together as one record the entire time Therefore, all expenses and effort to continue to receive their protection by not letting anything merge with her prior record was a lie. The costs to re-establish her life and keep her record clear were 'on her dime.' Without a work or credit history, the costs were high and damages in every part of her life were severe. After so many changes she was out of financial and professional options to start her life over one more time. Their only question: "**We just want to know how did you come through all of this and not commit suicide?**" Her answer was simple: "**God.**"

Clearly, she was done following all of their instructions and getting nowhere. Each time the fraud was supposed to be watched on her prior record and kept separate from her current record, it was not kept separate. Plus, code words they required and assigned with each ID change appear as aliases, so she appeared to be the fraudulent one.

Her merged record was accessible to anyone doing a credit or background check. It rendered her helpless for obtaining credit or employment from the world. All of the fraud committed by the Identity thieves is accessible so anyone checking on her background details would not see the record she stated and trusted was her one, clear record. Instead, people and businesses saw pages and pages of fraud so when she was told 'inconsistent record' each time she was not paid for her work, she had no idea what was going on.

God provided the wisdom and after five years of researching and providing the facts to the agents, the economic fraud division Deputy DA was arrested, convicted and sentenced on felony fraud.

She had already researched the fraud crimes and provided the facts to the agents. She did not know the truth: the agents lied. When she presented the list of errors to the agents, instead of taking one step to help her or clear her record the agents erased her from the system.

Sheila thanks God that her Lord and Savior stepped in and provided His wisdom and word of knowledge to help her figure out and know the truth: how the citizens, plus the credit, financial, and government systems are vulnerable due to policies allowing ID theft fraud to link to legal citizens while ID theft crimes continue without pursuing or prosecuting the criminals unless the name is already on a terrorist list. God reminded Sheila our identity as believers is in Christ: Ephesians 1:4-5, 2:10, along with a long list of scriptures.

God provided the facts and the connections for Sheila to write the Talking Points Memo for the Senate Banking & Finance Committee which they used to develop a new credit bureau and second ID Theft law signed on July 15, 2004.

In the midst of the many debacles and repeated, complete devastation, God has made a way. God has helped Sheila to re-direct all past knowledge into a new career.

Through global travel arranged by God, Sheila became recognized as an International Leadership, Balanced Life Coach. She is known to impact the life of each participant in corporations and conferences around the world. Her unique tools and techniques evoke immediate, positive, bottom-line strategies because they include the wisdom of God.

Her ID theft story regarding the two decades of devastation is briefly described within a film script and a non-fiction book, **Vulnerable: The Identity Factor.**

During the same two decades, God provided wisdom for her coaching tools and techniques which impact thousands of conference and seminar participants, business leaders, owners and their management teams on each continent.

Due to her dynamic leadership style, staff members and customers immediately recognize the changes in their life, their business, and the positive impact upon their family, peers, industry, and community. Relationships are blessed.

Due to God's word of knowledge being provided, participants consistently acknowledge her ability to ignite dialogue and inquiry throughout their life or business. They are inspired and re-encouraged so leadership immediately emerges within each life and partnership, i.e., with each staff member, their family members, each customer, vendor, and expanding into powerful business relationships, partnerships, and specifically in establishing multiple, profitable strategic alliances (shifting our focus from all transactions being based upon the exchange of a world based currency / money to becoming successful as a community or industry by sharing resources, aka establishing strategic alliances) which have positively catapulted their life, family & business to the next level of success. Then, they are able to bless more people.

Her coaching techniques are based upon **God's Storehouse Principle.** Sheila developed the practical tools while God took her hand and brought her out of the depth of the debacles. She uses the process to help her clients within the same 'balanced life game board' format, causing clients to realize they are actually 'playing the game' in their own life. The simple format confirms that with bit of practice we can shift from world based processes to **God's Storehouse Principle** and live a full, 7/24 life.

Sheila delivers motivational speeches for corporations and conferences around the world. While traveling as a keynote speaker and seminar leader. A brief list of Sheila's speaking and coaching clients include:

- American Society of Training and Development
- EDS,
- WERC, NESRA, etc.
- Chevron

- Executive Forum
- The Executive Committee (TEC)
- Rotary and Kiwanis International, etc.
- National Insurance Brokers and Agents (NIBA)
- Society for Human Resources Management (SHRM)

Sheila has been featured and quoted on MSNBC, KCBS, CNN Industry Watch, and in Inc Magazine and The Business Cube.

She credits God for providing the wisdom and word of knowledge. The plans are God's plans and the success is based upon God's orchestration of the details.

God arranged a journey, confirming **It's A Faith Walk!** and Sheila recently released the book which includes about seven months of their three year adventure. Her faith walk is truly the result of letting God orchestrate her life, a journey which is God's plan for each of us and God's orchestration for Sheila confirms His plan is beyond our human comprehension.

She prays you will embark on a journey with God and be blessed when you live life per **God's Storehouse Principle**.

Her unique training program caused the American Federal Government to extend an annual contract to her, to provide God's wisdom within a business development course for the Defense industry.

The 100% success rate of the course provided automatic annual contract renewals for both the Defense and Aerospace industries, where industry participants, i.e., General Dynamics, Hughes and Lockheed, benefited.

Sheila has become a published author Her copyrighted course material became the basis of her business book:

Seven Step Business Plan
Foreword by Ken Blanchard
Distributed by Pelican Publishing

It has garnered international recognition. The book became a key part of the Buckminster Fuller Business School for Entrepreneurs program in Kuala Lumpur, Malaysia and Shenzhen, China. In addition, the European Union Chamber of Commerce requires her book within their core curriculum. The book has been translated into the Spanish Language and published in a Latin America edition.

Her *Balanced Life Game* includes her popular Keynote Conference topic: *Networking Through Six Degrees of Separation.*

Balanced Life Game and ***Vulnerable: The Identity Factor*** books are currently in negotiation with Pelican, the same publisher as ***Seven Step Business Plan***.

Sheila is a lifetime member of the San Diego Society for Human Resources Management (SHRM) and she has served on the boards of a long list of professional and community associations. She founded the industry panel and instructed three of the six core courses for the Management Certificate Program at the University of California, San Diego. She founded and operated a California Corporation after she further developed and directed both marketing and human resources departments for major corporations such as: PAC West, National Pen, AVCO and TraveLodge Int'l. She became a SHRM and Greater San Diego Industry Education Council board member while working in both Production & Industrial Relations at SONY Corporation. She chaired a Robotics in Warehousing project which resulted in spending time in each of the SONY plants in Japan. She chaired the first Western Regional Human Resources Conference held in San Diego, California.

She was an Education major at Augustana College, became certified in Telecommunications at Palomar College, obtained a BA degree in Management from Pepperdine University and she is an MBA candidate, Southern Illinois University.

Sheila is actively engaged in numerous community and charitable activities. She has also enjoyed participating in her special interest, high-speed car rallies especially when they are conducted on California mountain routes.

Sheila looks forward to hearing the details of your testimony for the truth about our daily life is **It's A Faith Walk!** and it is a glorious journey when we understand how to bring it all together when we fellowship in one accord and know that we know we are functioning in daily life according to **God's Storehouse Principle.**

Email: hisbest4usorders@gmail.com

Web site: http://hisbest4us.org

Facebook: HISBest4us

Use the subject line: **God's Storehouse Principle.**

Aimee Semple McPherson, founder of the global Four Square Church which had spread to 67 countries during her lifetime: *"Give your heart to God. Come and help me. With salvation, baptism of the Holy Spirit and divine healing ... Are you born again? Does anyone know that you're saved? Let the world know that you're on the Lord's side. If you're a soldier of the King and a soldier of the cross, then fight the good fight of faith. Grow up to be men and women, filled with the spirit and glorifying God ... be willing to live according to* Acts 2:4. And they were all filled with the Holy Spirit and began to speak with other tongues, as the Spirit gave them utterance. ... *and lay down their lives for the sake of the Gospel."*

Matthew Barnett *"Faith is believing that God is going to take you places before you even get there."*

Kenneth Copeland *"God's plan for your life is bigger than everything coming against it."*

Oswald Chambers *"Faith is deliberate confidence in the character of God whose ways you may not understand at the time."*

John G. Lake *"Do you know what prayer is? It is not begging God for this and that. The first thing we have to do is to get you beggars to quit begging until a little faith moves in your souls."*

Corrie Ten Boom *"Never be afraid to trust an unknown future to a known God."*

Dare To Believe, Then Command

Smith Wigglesworth – 1919

"Verily, verily, I say unto you; He that believeth on Me, the works that I do shall he do also: and greater works than these shall he do; because I go unto My Father. And whatsoever ye shall ask in My name, that will I do, that the Father may be glorified in the Son. If ye shall ask any thing in My name, I will do it." John 14:12-14.

Jesus is speaking here, and the Spirit of God can take these words of His and make them real to us. "He that believeth on Me... greater works than these shall he do." What a word! Is it true? If you want the truth, where will you get it? "Thy word is truth," Christ said to the Father. When you take up God's Word you get the truth. God is not the author of confusion or error, but He sends forth His light and truth to lead us into His holy habitation, where we receive a revelation of the truth like unto the noon day in all its clearness.

The Word of God works effectually in us as we believe it. It changes us and brings us into new fellowship with the Father, with the Son, and with the Holy Spirit, into a holy communion, into an unwavering faith, into a mighty assurance, and it will make us partakers of the very nature and likeness of God as we receive His great and exceeding precious promises and believe them. Faith cometh by hearing, and hearing by the Word of God. Faith is the operative power.

We read that Christ opened the understanding of His disciples, and He will open up our understanding and our hearts and will show us wonderful things that we should never know but for the mighty revelation and enlightenment of the Spirit that He gives to us.

I do not know of any greater words than those found in Romans 4:16, "Therefore it is of faith, that it might be by grace." Grace is God's benediction coming right down to you, and when you open the door to Him—that is an act of faith—He does all you want and will fulfill all your desires. "It is of faith, that it might be by grace." You open the way for God to work as you believe His Word, and God will come in and supply your every need all along the way.

Our Lord Jesus said to His disciples and He says to us in this passage in the 14th of John, "You have seen Me work and you know how I work. You shall do the very same things that I am doing, and greater things shall you do, because I am going to the Father, and as you make petition in My name I will work. I will do what you ask, and by this the Father shall be glorified."

Did any one ever work as He did? I do not mean His carpentering. I refer to His work in the hearts of the people. He drew them to Him. They came with their needs, with their sicknesses, with their oppression, and He relieved them all. This royal Visitor, who came from the Father to express His love, talked to men, spent time with them in their homes, found out their every need. He went about doing good and healing all who were oppressed of the devil, and He said to them and He says to us, "You see what I have been doing, healing the sick, relieving the oppressed, casting out demons. The works that I do shall ye do also." Dare you believe? Will you take up the work that He left and carry it on?

"He that believeth on Me!" What is this? What does it mean? How can just believing bring these things to pass? What virtue is there in it? There is virtue in these words because He declares them. If we will receive this word and declare it, the greater works shall be accomplished. This is a positive declaration of His, "He that believeth on Me, greater works than these shall he do," but unbelief has hindered our progress in the realm of the spiritual.

Put away unbelief. Open your heart to God's grace. Then God will come in and place in you a definite faith. He wants to remove every obstruction that is in the world before you. By His grace He will enable you to be so established in His truth, so strong in the Lord and in the power of His might, that whatever comes across your path to obstruct you, you can arise in divine power and rebuke and destroy it.

It is a matter of definite and clear understanding between us and God. To recognize that Christ has a life force to put into us, changes everything that we dare to *believe* it will change. He that believes that Jesus is the Christ overcomes the world. Because we believe that Jesus is the Christ, the essence of divine life is in us by faith and causes a perfect separation between us and the world. We have no room for sin. It is a joyful thing for us to be doing that which is right. He will cause that abundance of grace to so flow into our hearts that sin shall not have dominion over us. Sin shall not have dominion; nor sickness, nor affliction. "He that believeth"—he that dares to believe—he that dares to trust—will see victory over every oppression of the enemy.

A needy creature came to me in a meeting, all withered and wasted. He had no hope. There was absolute death in his eyes. He was so helpless he had to have some one on each side to bear him up. He came to me and said in a whisper, "Can you help me?" Will Jesus answer? "He that believeth on Me, the works that I do shall he do also; and greater works than these…. Behold, I give you power… over all the power of the enemy." These are the words of our Lord Jesus. It is not our word but the word of the Lord, and as this word is in us He can make it like a burning passion in us. We make the Word of God as we believe it our own. We receive the Word and we have the very life of Christ in us. We become supernatural by the power of God. We find this power working through every part of our being.

Now Christ gives us something besides faith. He gives us something to make faith effectual. Whatsoever you desire, if you believe in your heart you shall have. Christ said, "Have faith in God. For verily I say unto you, That whosoever shall say unto this mountain, Be thou removed, and be thou cast into the sea; and shall not doubt in his heart, but shall believe that those things which he saith shall come to pass; he shall have whatsoever he saith. Therefore I say unto you, What things soever ye desire, when ye pray, believe that ye receive them, and ye shall have them." Mark 11:22-24. Whatsoever he saith! Dare to say in faith and it shall be done. These things have been promised by Christ and He does not lie.

This afflicted man stood before me helpless and withered. He had had cancer in his stomach. The physicians had operated upon him to take away the cancer from the stomach, but complications had arisen with the result that no food could enter the man's stomach. He could not swallow anything. So in order to keep him alive they made a hole in his stomach and put in a tube about nine inches long with a cup at the top, and he was fed with liquid through this tube. For three months he had been just kept alive but was like a skeleton.

What was I to say to him? "If thou wouldest believe, thou shouldest see the glory of God."

Here was the word of Christ, "He that believeth on me, the works that I do shall he do also, and greater works than these shall he do; because I go unto My Father." The Word of God is truth. Christ is with the Father and grants us our requests, and makes these things manifest, if we believe. What should I do in the presence of a case like this? "Believe the Word." So I believed the Word which says, "He shall have whatsoever he saith." Mark 11:23. I said, "Go home, and have a good supper." He said, "I cannot swallow."

"Go home, and have a good supper," I repeated. "On the authority of the Word of God I say it. Christ says that he that believes that these things which he says shall come to pass he shall have whatsoever he says. So I say, Go home in the name of Jesus, and have a good supper."

He went home. Supper was prepared. Many times he had had food in his mouth but had always been forced to spit it out again. But I dared to believe that he would be able to swallow that night. So that man filled his mouth full as he had done before, and because some one dared to believe God's Word and said to him, "You shall have a good supper in the name of Jesus," when he chewed his food it went down in the normal way into his stomach, and he ate until he was quite satisfied.

He and his family went to bed filled with joy. The next morning when they arose they were filled with the same joy.

Life had begun again. Naturally he looked down to see the hole that had been made in his stomach by the physicians. But God knew that he did not want two holes, and so when God opened the normal passage He closed the other hole in his stomach. This is the kind of God we have all the time, a God who knows, a God who acts, and brings things to pass when we believe. Dare to believe, and then dare to speak and you shall have whatsoever you say if you doubt not.

A woman came to me one night and inquired, "Can I hear again? Is it possible for me to hear again? I have had several operations and the drums of my ears have been taken away." I said, "If God has not forgotten how to make drums for ears you can hear again." Do you think God has forgotten? What does God forget? He forgets our sins, when we are forgiven, but He has not forgotten how to make drums for ears.

Not long ago the power of God was very much upon a meeting that I was holding. I was telling the people that they could be healed without my going to them. If they would rise up I would pray and the Lord would heal. There was a man who put up his hand. I said, "Cannot that man rise?" The folks near him said he could not, and lifted him hp. The Lord healed him the ribs that were broken were knit together again and were healed.

There was such faith in the place that a little girl cried out, "Please, gentleman, come to me." You could not see her, she was so small. The mother said, "My little girl wants you to come." So I went down there to this child, who although fourteen years of age was very small. She said with tears streaming down her face, "Will you pray for me?" I said, "Dare you believe?" She said, "O yes." I prayed and placed my hands on her head in the name of Jesus.

"Mother," she said, "I am being healed. Take these things off—take them all off." The mother loosed straps and bands and then the child said, "Mother, I am sure I am healed. Take these off." She had straps on her legs and an iron on her foot about 3½ inches deep. She asked her mother to unstrap her. Her mother took off the straps. There were not many people with dry eyes as they saw that girl walk about with legs just as normal as when she was born. God healed her right away. What did it? She had cried, "Please, gentleman, come to me," and her longing was coupled with faith. May the Lord help us to be just like a simple child.

God has hidden these things from the wise and prudent, but He reveals them to babes. There is something in childlike faith in God that makes us dare to believe, and then to act. Whatever there is in your life that is bound, the name of Jesus and the power of that name will break it if you will only believe. Christ says, "If ye shall ask any thing in My name, I will do it." God will be glorified in Christ when you receive the overflowing life that comes from Christ in response to your faith.

Dare to believe. Do you think that truth is put into the Word to mock you? Don't you see that God really means that you should live in the world to relieve the oppression of the world? God answers us that we shall be quickened, be molded afresh, that the Word of God shall change everything that needs to be changed, both in us and in others, as we dare to believe and as we command things to be done. "Whosoever shall say unto this mountain, Be thou removed, and be thou cast into the sea; and shall not doubt in his heart, but shall believe that those things which he saith shall come to pass, he shall have whatsoever he saith."

Published in the Pentecostal Evangel on March 30, 1940

America was Founded upon Faith as the Path to Freedom and Liberty

Faith Monument

On the main pedestal stands the heroic figure of "Faith" with her right hand pointing toward heaven and her left hand clutching the Bible. Upon the four buttresses also are seated figures emblematical of the principles upon which the Pilgrims founded their Commonwealth, each having a symbol referring to the Bible that "Faith" possesses; counter-clockwise from the feet of "Faith" are Morality, Law, Education, and Liberty. Each was carved from a solid block of granite, posed in the sitting position upon chairs with a high relief on either side of minor characteristics. Under "Morality" stand "Prophet" and "Evangelist"; under "Law" stand "Justice" and "Mercy"; under "Education" are "Youth" and "Wisdom"; and under "Liberty" stand "Tyranny Overthrown" and "Peace". On the face of the buttresses, beneath these figures are high reliefs in marble, representing scenes from Pilgrim history. Under "Morality" is "Embarcation"; under "Law" is "Treaty"; under "Education" is "Compact"; and under "Freedom" is "Landing". Upon the four faces of the main pedestal are large panels for records. The front panel is inscribed as follows:

"National Monument to the Forefathers: Erected by a grateful people in remembrance of their labors, sacrifices and sufferings for the cause of civil and religious liberty." The right and left panels contain the names of those who came over in the *Mayflower*.

The rear panel, which was not engraved until recently, contains a quote from Governor William Bradford's famous history, *Of Plymouth Plantation*:

"Thus out of small beginnings greater things have been produced by His hand that made all things of nothing and gives being to all things that are; and as one small candle may light a thousand, so the light here kindled hath shone unto many, yea in some sort to our whole nation; let the glorious name of Jehovah have all praise."

Made in the USA
Middletown, DE
04 May 2022